A C++

**Prentice Hall Series in Innovative Technology**

Dennis R. Allison, David J. Farber, and Bruce D. Shriver          *Series Advisors*

**Kane**          *MIPS RISC Architecture*
**Rose**          *The Open Book: A Practical Perspective on OSI*
**Rose**          *The Simple Book: An Introduction to Management of TCP/IP-based internets*
**Shapiro**          *A C++ Toolkit*
**Slater**          *Microprocessor-Based Design*
**Wirfs-Brock, Wilkerson, and Weiner**          *Designing Object-Oriented Software*

# A
# C++
# Toolkit

Jonathan Shapiro

*HaL Computer Systems, Inc.*

*Prentice Hall, Englewood Cliffs, New Jersey 07632*

Library of Congress Cataloging-in-Publication Data

Shapiro, Jonathan S.
    A C++ tool kit / Jonathan S. Shapiro.
        p.    cm.
    Includes bibliographical references and index.
    ISBN 0-13-127663-8
    1. C`` (Computer program language)   I. Title.
QA76.73.C153S43  1991
005.26--dc20                                               90-43588
                                                          CIP

Editorial/production supervision: *Brendan M. Stewart*
Manufacturing buyers: *Kelly Behr* and *Susan Brunke*

Published by Prentice-Hall, Inc.
A Division of Simon & Schuster
Englewood Cliffs, New Jersey 07632

The author and publisher of this book have used their best efforts in preparing the software programs listed in this book. These efforts include the development, research and testing of the theories and programs to determine their effectiveness. The author and publisher make no warranty of any kind, expressed or implied, with regard to the programs in this book. The author and publisher shall not be liable in any event for incidental or consequential damages in connection with, or arising out of, the furnishing, performance, or use of these programs.

You may use and redistribute the programs and code fragments in this book without royaltee or fee, provided that the following notice is included in the associated documentation and in the online program information display: Portions of this work are derived from *A C++ Toolkit,* which is Copyright © 1991 by Jonathan S. Shapiro, and are used with permission. *A C++ Toolkit* is published by Prentice Hall, Inc.

The publisher offers discounts on this book when ordered in bulk quantities. For more information, write: Special Sales/College Marketing, Prentice-Hall, Inc., College Technical and Reference Division, Englewood Cliffs, New Jersey 07632

Printed in the United States of America
10  9  8  7  6  5  4  3  2

ISBN 0-13-127663-8

Prentice-Hall International (UK) Limited, *London*
Prentice-Hall of Australia Pty. Limited, *Sydney*
Prentice-Hall Canada Inc., *Toronto*
Prentice-Hall Hispanoamericana, S.A., *Mexico*
Prentice-Hall of India Private Limited, *New Delhi*
Prentice-Hall of Japan, Inc., *Tokyo*
Simon & Schuster Asia Pte. Ltd., *Singapore*
Editora Prentice-Hall do Brasil, Ltda., *Rio de Janeiro*

# Contents

## Complete Classes                                            **(continued)**

## **Index**                                                       **227**

*If builders built buildings the way programmers write programs, the first woodpecker would destroy civilization.*
*— Anonymous*

# Preface

When I first started using C++ in 1986, the language was still changing at a brutal pace, and there weren't any books for newcomers to the language. Since that time, C++ has stabilized a bit, and several books have come onto the market that teach C++ programming to people who already know C. However, these books focus on C++ as a language rather than as a problem solving tool. My assumption is that C programmers already know most of the C++ language. The challenge is in learning to use it, and the best way to learn to use a programming language is by example.

C++ is not an easy language to use well. At first glance the language seems very similar to C, but this appearance is deceptive. On the one hand, C++ has many object-oriented features, and a good C++ programmer will make heavy use of them. On the other hand, C++ is derived from C, and there are places where procedural programming techniques are appropriate. Finally, there are places where the need to support C features prevents C++ from supporting object-oriented features as well as one might like, and a surprising number of programs will run up against these problems in one way or another.

Most books on programming in C++ focus on two things: the basics of object-oriented programming and the basics of C++. This book focuses instead on the broader problem of using C++ to construct reusable tools, and presents some of the techniques and approaches that make C++ a good language for building such software tools. The approach of this book is to introduce a way of thinking about reusable programming  This approach is reinforced by a number of examples that illustrate how these ideas are applied.

This is a second generation book about C++. It makes use of the second major version of the language, C++ 2.0, and reflects the fact that our understanding of how to use the language has matured since the early books were written.

*A C++ Toolkit* is divided into four sections. The first section discusses the problem of software reuse, and how object-oriented programming languages can help. It provides a reader's guide to the C++ language for newcomers, and presents some easily understood classes to introduce some of the flavor of the language. Most important, it establishes a conceptual model for what it means to build reusable software tools.

The second section is the body of the book. Each chapter in this section provides a complete, reusable tool that has proven useful in my own programming projects. In some cases, the tools are further explored or generalized by subsequent chapters.

Storage management and performance tuning are important parts of C++ programming. Section three provides some techniques for managing memory and tuning the performance of C++ applications. It also presents a peek at some forthcoming features in C++: exception handling and templates.

The final section contains listings of each class presented in the book in its final form. This is intended to make it easier to understand the overall structure of any given class. In addition, it provides a single place to work from if you wish to use any of these classes in your own programs.

Each chapter ends with a set of exercises. The primary purpose of these exercises is to provoke you into serious thought about the issues they raise. The exercises are also intended to reinforce the material in the chapter or to lay the groundwork for subsequent chapters.

The source code is intended to be reused, and you are free to copy it into your programs provided you follow the terms of the copyright notice in the front of the book.  If you have any questions, or you think your need isn't covered, please contact Prentice Hall.

## Credits and Thanks

A large number of people deserve recognition for their help in making this book happen.  Without them, this effort would never have gotten off the ground.

Bjarne Stroustrup exhibited more patience in dealing with me than I probably deserved, and of course invented the language on which *A C++ Toolkit* is based.  He is a remarkable individual, and I wish that more people took the time to consider how good a job he has done before they tell him how it was done wrong, insisting that their way is better.

Bell Laboratories has had a long history of focusing on tool construction. Brian Kernighan and P.J. Plauger wrote *Software Tools in Pascal*, which was the first programming book I ever encountered that I felt was a good book for a beginning programmer.  *Software Tools* isn't about Pascal.  It's about programming, which is why I like it.  John Bentley is the author of a series of columns entitled *Programming Pearls*, which have been republished as books of the same name.  I have tried to retain much of their flavor in *A C++ Toolkit*.

Roger Faulkner was the author of something called the "Record Management" classes, a memory management system that formed the basis for the reference-counted pointer classes presented here.  Together we are better designers than either of us is alone, and most of the ideas in this book reflect the improvement of his suggestions and criticisms over the years.  Roger has also been a personal friend for a number of years.

Dennis Allison of Stanford University, and Karen Gettman and Paul Becker of Prentice Hall are the ones who finally convinced me to undertake the writing of this book when I could have been earning a living instead.  Dennis is an ongoing source of interesting conversations.  Next time he suggests I write a book I think I will ask him to do the typing.

Several folks at Silicon Graphics, Inc. pitched in when it finally all got rolling. Lia Adams, Bean Anderson, Dave Ciemiewicz, Andrew Myers, and John Wilkinson critiqued and improved many parts of this book. Kipp and Andrew were working on a C++ tools library about the same time this book finally came together, and I would like to think that there was some cross fertilization of ideas between us. Certainly, their ideas have influenced me.

By far the person who invested the most effort in the book outside of myself was Harry Max, who copy edited the book in his spare time. Copy editing is a difficult and thankless job, and Harry's efforts to make my writing readable were indispensable. He is a terrific person to work with, and I hope I will soon get a chance to return the favor.

Most of all, my family and Diane Carlson, for putting up with the demon who occasionally borrows my body for fits of authorship and other insanity that runs late into the night.

## Disclaimer

My goal, first and foremost, has been to make this book useful. While I have done my best to make *A C++ Toolkit* accurate, it is inevitable that some number of mistakes have managed to make it into print. The best efforts of the many people who have helped make the book more accurate will not have caught them all. If you should come across an error, I hope that you will share it with me via Prentice Hall so that it can be corrected in future editions of the book. I am also interested in hearing your suggestions for how *A C++ Toolkit* might be improved or extended to better serve your needs.

Jonathan Shapiro
Menlo Park, California

## Exercises

1. Why are you reading this book? What do you hope to get out of it?

2. What is "object-oriented programming?"

3. What are the steps you go through when you design a new data structure?

4. Who is Adele Goldberg?

5. Buy a friend a copy of this book.

# A C++ Toolkit

*My thesis is that the software industry is weakly founded, and that one aspect of this weakness is the absence of a software components subindustry.*

— *M.D. McIlroy*

# The Software Crisis

When I first joined Bell Laboratories in 1981, the signs of a software crisis were already upon us. It would be several years before the implications in the large of these problems were recognized, but a single example may make the point:

The UNIX® system in 1981 supported several editors: *ed*, a very simple editor whose origins go back to the first editors developed at the MIT AI Lab; *ex*, an enhanced version of *ed* that provided for more sophisticated kinds of editing operations and had generally better support for editing within a line; *vi*, a screen-oriented editor developed from *ex* by Bill Joy at the University of California at Berkeley as part of the BSD UNIX release; and *jim*, an editor put together by Rob Pike for an internal terminal that was later to reach the public as the Teletype 630 multiwindowing terminal.

*Jim* was a much later development, and part of its purpose was to experiment with new ideas for editing. The other three editors, *ed*, *ex*, and *vi*, that should, in theory, have shared a lot of common behavior. They were based on the same source code and did essentially similar things. Indeed, a few commands did work similarly, or at least seemed to from the perspective of the less advanced user.

Consider, as an example, an operation that editors are called on to do very frequently: search for a particular piece of text or pattern of text in a file. This is called *regular expression search*, and each editor has the capability to do this type of searching. Each, of course, was subtly or grossly different from the others, depending on what you wanted to do.

Several other UNIX commands provided regular expression search capabilities. The *grep* command was designed to search through files for patterns without having to invoke an editor. There was also *fgrep* (**f**ast grep), which was specialized to look only for particular text strings in files. Later, there was *egrep* (**e**xtended grep), which supported a more general class of patterns than *grep* did.

*Awk*, of course, built on these previous versions, extending the existing mechanisms for greater flexibility. Then there was the command processor, *sh* (or in some environments, *csh*, which had yet another pattern matcher), which did still another variety of pattern matching for filename processing.

If you begin to find the enumeration of different pattern-matching mechanisms available on the UNIX system in 1981 somewhat appalling, I have made my point. The development on these tools proceeded over the course of a number of years, and each was slightly or grossly incompatible with the mechanisms of the others. In each case, a good argument can be made that the differences are desirable. This still leaves the end user of the UNIX system needing to know nine different sets of rules for how to search for things, depending on which command is used.

## 1.1   The Failure of Libraries

In recognition of the fact that variety isn't always the spice of life, it was decided to build a library routine that future commands could use to do their pattern matching so that the world seen by the user would start to be more consistent. Eventually, two different library routines, *regex* and *regexp*, were developed (the second because the first didn't work very well), which managed to be subtly incompatible with all of the previous regular expression processors.

No interesting program has ever used either of these library packages! Every program that does sophisticated pattern matching on the UNIX system today uses one of two time-honored techniques to do the job:

- steal the code from *ex* and modify it to meet the particular demands of your application,

- write your own pattern matcher from scratch.

The expense of such solutions, both in terms of development and support cost and in terms of the difficulty of use seen by the end user, is simply awesome. The question to be asked here is: "Why didn't the library routines work?" After all, the idea of libraries is to encapsulate functionality in a common place so that everyone can make use of it.

There are two reasons that the library scheme failed. The first is that pattern matching is like religion. Most people like their own and don't want to change. The choice is more a matter of faith than of reason.

The second reason is more important: a procedure library cannot capture all of the notions that are needed to address the problem of pattern matching in a way that is general enough for use by all of the tools that need to do pattern matching. Regular expression search requires a number of fairly complicated abstractions:

| | |
|---|---|
| *regular expressions* | The description of the text you are searching for. |
| *regular expression compiler* | The program that turns the regular expression into an efficient form that can be used by the regular expression interpreter. |
| *regular expression interpreter* | The engine that actually does the searching for us. |
| *buffer* | The body of text that we intend to search. |

For the problem of regular expression matching, the difficulty lies in the meaning of "buffer." Each of the applications in question performs a specialized task, and implements its buffers in whatever way is most efficient for that task. No two buffer implementations are exactly alike. The challenge is to specify the interface between the buffer and the regular expression interpreter, so that each application can provide the functionality that the regular expression engine needs.

## 1.2    The Object-Oriented Approach

From a technical perspective, the problem with the procedure libraries is that the programmer doesn't have control over the right things. A procedure interface talks about datatypes and operations, not about abstractions and interfaces. If you don't have the right datatypes, or your model for these datatypes is slightly different from the model used by the person who wrote the library, you are pretty much out of luck.

Consider the regular expression library problem. What is needed is a "base" buffer that specifies the interface to the buffer needed by the regular expression interpreter but doesn't prevent the different editors and tools from providing their own detailed implementations of the buffer abstraction. Different editors could then provide specialized versions of buffers suited to their own particular needs.

Object-oriented programming languages are an attempt to solve exactly this sort of problem. These languages focus on being able to do four things:

- Specify a complete abstract description of the kind of "thing" you need to work with.

- Build new abstractions by composing or specializing existing ones, promoting reuse.

- Describe the interactions that your abstraction knows how to make with the surrounding environment.

- Implement these abstractions in a modular way.

C++ is an attempt, largely successful, to unify these ideas with a wide existing base of C software. Object-oriented languages have had a hard time gaining widespread acceptance, partly because until C++ they have all required abandoning or rewriting existing code, and partly because they have all imposed a substantial performance penalty.[1]

When designing programs in C++, the questions to keep in mind are:

- What are the different kinds of entities that my program needs to manipulate?

- How do these entities interact?

- What opportunities are there to take advantage of work that others have already done?

- How can I design my abstractions to be general enough that others can take advantage of them? If you prefer, how can I find the right abstraction for the job?

Note carefully a couple of questions that are *not* on the list:

- How can I get the last ounce of performance out of the code I am writing?

- How little can I do to solve this problem?

To use object-oriented languages most effectively, a programmer must take a long term view of software development. Invest extra time now to avoid investing it again later. Good object-oriented design focuses on reuse.

## 1.3  Designing for Reuse

The term "software reuse" is abused in so many different contexts that it is easy to wonder if it has any meaning at all. Different people want

---

[1]   There is, of course, somewhat more to it than that. Most object oriented languages require *garbage collection*, a technique for dynamic storage management. Until the recent wide acceptance of incremental generational garbage collectors, garbage collection has been slow, and it has imposed overhead on programs in unpredictable ways. Recent technology advances have rendered this issue essentially moot, but old memories die slowly.

different things out of software reuse, so they think about reuse in different terms.

Large companies have a considerable stake in keeping their software private. The sad state of copyright and software patent law means that software houses are protected only by keeping the details of their software completely secret. This presents a catch-22. As software houses, these companies understand the advantages to letting other people build on their tool sets; if I can convince you to build a product with my tool kit, and I can charge a royalty for it, I stand to make a fair amount of money.

Our current understanding of software isn't yet sophisticated enough to be able to meet the goal of binary reuse. One of the major reasons for the success of the X Window System, GNU EMACS, the Andrew Toolkit, and other widely used software systems is that they are available in source form. Very often, a class from the X Athena Widgets tool kit is exactly what I need. More often small enhancements are required.

In short, we still don't know enough about reuse for binary reuse to be practical. Software reuse is still a source-level phenomenon. If this is so, what are the advantages to object-oriented programming languages?

Programming languages do not control the way you program in a direct way. Their influence is more subtle. Loops can be written in languages that have a `goto` statement. They are easier to write in languages that have looping constructs. More important, they are easier to understand. Most C++ compilers today generate C code. Since this is true, it is clear that we could do object-oriented programming in C. What C++ provides is a formal set of language constructs that make it easier to build these objects. A class declaration is a complete statement about the data contained by the object, the functions that operate on the object, and which clients are entitled to use the functions and data. The interface *encapsulates* the class.

A direct result of this is that C++ source code is easier to reuse than C source code, because there is no need to hunt through a large body of source to find all of the functions you need. The definition of a class tells you exactly what it does and doesn't do. Because a class encapsulates a complete working unit of code, classes can be lifted out as a unit and modified to suit a new set of needs.

Encapsulation has another interesting consequence. Because classes can control which clients can use various parts of the class, the class interface is a statement of all of the things a client can possibly know about the class. It describes an *abstraction*. The class implementor is free to rearrange the internals of the class in any way that seems appropriate, including replacing them wholesale.

Because object-oriented languages permit us to build abstractions and specialize them, object-oriented design focuses on building general solutions and specializing these solutions to meet specific needs. Whether or not the specific version of an object will be of use to someone else, the general form will almost certainly provide a basis for solving someone else's problem.

Good object-oriented designers focus on building *tools*, components that other programmers can use to solve problems similar to ours. Building software tools is one of the major focuses of this book. Each chapter presents several general tools along with specific applications of these tools to solve particular problems. By the end of the book, the tool set that we have built up is sufficiently powerful that we can use it to implement solutions to some surprisingly complicated problems with very little new code.

Designing general solutions is hard. It requires stepping back from the problem at hand and looking at the broader picture. It has been my experience that this process is best learned by example.

## Exercises

1. How many different kinds of regular expression processor should the UNIX system have?

2. What customer is impacted by having too many regular expression matching languages? Why wasn't this important to the implementors of the UNIX® system editors?

3. Ken Thompson has been heard to say that if he had it to do all over again, the only change he would make to the UNIX system is to change the name of the `creat()` system call to `create()`. What does he mean?

4. What are the key items that make software reuse possible? If you prefer, what are the properties of the programming language(s) you use now that make software reuse hard?

5. How many times have you written code that implements a singly-linked or doubly-linked list? Why?

6. In the description of *vi*, *ed*, and *ex*, I asserted that there were good reasons to enhance the regular expression facility in each editor. Enhancements always represent a trade-off between leveraging what the user already knows and increasing the number of things they have to learn to use your product. What are the criteria that should be used to determine if an enhancement is justified?

7. Once you decide to do an enhancement in a new product, should the new feature be retrofitted to existing software to ensure compatibility? Why or why not?

*The only way to learn a new programming*
*language is by writing programs in it.*
*— Brian Kernighan*

2

# A Reader's Guide to C++

C++ is in most regards an extension of C. It provides a number of features to make general programming easier to do and easier to maintain. This chapter provides a brief summary of these extensions and features to help you if you are still learning C++. If you are a newcomer to the language, I recommend starting with a book such as *The C++ Primer,* by Stan Lippman, or *Programming in C++*, by Steve Dewhurst and Kathy Stark. This book assumes that you already know C++.

## 2.1 Argument Prototypes

The first extension to C that C++ provides is argument prototypes. When a function is declared using prototypes, the argument types appear in the declaration. This lets the compiler verify that the arguments passed to a function agree in number and type with the arguments that the function expects. Prototypes also provides the necessary information for doing *type safe linking*, which makes it possible to verify that all declarations and uses of a function agree.

From a textual standpoint, the change in the way functions are defined in C++ as compared to C is small:

C version

```
main(argc, argv)
  int argc;
  const char *argv[];
{
   // ...
}
```

C++ version

```
main(int argc,
     const char *argv[])
{
   // ...
}
```

Function declarations also make use of argument prototypes. Consider the declaration of `printf()`:

C version

```
extern int
printf();
```

C++ version

```
extern int
printf(const char *, ...);
```

The traditional C version simply asserts that `printf()` is a function. The C++ declaration in addition specifies that `printf()` takes a first argument that is a pointer to characters that `printf()` will not modify, followed by an unspecified number (0 or more) of arguments whose type is not known in advance.

Arguments are also necessary for function pointer declarations in C++:

C version

```
extern int (*pfi)();
```

C++ version

```
extern int (*pfi)(int);
```

C++ argument prototypes were adopted into the ANSI C standard. There is, however, one major difference between argument prototypes as specified in ANSI C and argument prototypes as specified in C++. In ANSI C the declaration

```
extern int f();
```

means "a function returning an integer and taking an unspecified set of arguments." In C++ it means "a function returning an integer that takes *no* arguments." The ANSI C standard advises that this usage is obsolete. It is retained for backwards compatibility with existing C code. A better declaration is:

```
extern int f(void);
```

Unlike C, which does not enforce function call type checking, it is an error in C++ code to call a function before you have declared it.

## 2.2 Type Safe Linking

C++ makes use of the function prototype to provide type safe linking. When you call a function in C++, C++ changes the function's name to include information about the argument types:

| C++ Code | Output |
|---|---|
| ```extern int CurrentTime(void); // ... i = CurrentTime();``` | ```extern int _11CurrentTime_Fv(); // ... i = _11CurrentTime_Fv();``` |

If the actual definition of the function expected an integer to be passed, its name would be different in the output code, and the linker would complain that the function `CurrentTime(void)` was undefined.

## 2.3 Function Overloading

Requiring arguments to be declared permits C++ to allow function names to be reused, because the argument types can be used to resolve which version of a function to use. Thus, we could define a set of `print()` functions that do the right thing depending on the type of the argument.

```
void print(int i)
{
    printf("%d", i);
}

void print(float f)
{
    printf("%f", f);
}
```

```
void print(mystruct& s)
{
    // ... your interpretation here...
}
// ...
```

Because the function declarations include the argument types, C++ can ensure that the right version of the function is called, even if the function definition and the caller are in different source files.

## 2.4    References

Another feature introduced in C++ is references. A *reference* is an alias for another object. References are used in two contexts: in function argument prototypes, where they are similar to Pascal `var` parameters, and in C++ code, where they permit name aliases to be created. A reference argument can be implemented in C by declaring the argument as a pointer argument and taking the address of the argument at the call site:

| C version | C++ version |
|---|---|
| `typedef struct mystruct_s`<br>`        mystruct_s;` | `// no typedef needed` |
| `int f(mystruct_s *);`<br>`// ...` | `int f(mystruct_s&);`<br>`// ...` |
| `mystruct_s mystruct;`<br>`i = f(&mystruct);` | `mystruct_s mystruct;`<br>`i = f(mystruct);` |
| `void`<br>`f(mystruct_s *s)`<br>`{`<br>`    (*s).field = value;`<br>`}` | `void`<br>`f(mystruct_s& s)`<br>`{`<br>`    s.field = value;`<br>`}` |

The difference is that in the C version you must explicitly take the address of the argument, and the function must explicitly dereference it in the function. In C++, both of these are handled automatically. Note also that in C++ the `struct` keyword is not needed in the declaration, since C++ structure tag names and type names are in the same name space.

References can be used as a way to make argument passing more efficient in a way that is transparent to the user. For example, these two declarations are indistinguishable from the caller's perspective:

By-value version                    By-reference version

```
int f(const mystruct_s);        int f(const mystruct_s&);
```

The same object is passed at the call site, and `f()` is not permitted to modify the structure in either case.

From the standpoint of implementation, there are two important differences. The by-reference version passes a pointer to the object, while the by-value version requires copying the entire structure onto the stack and then removing it when the function returns.

Perhaps more important, the by-value version creates a temporary, for which a constructor and destructor must be called. We shall return to the topic of constructors and destructors in a moment.

The other context in which references can be used is in initializations, where they create aliases:

```
mystruct_s& s_ref = s;
```

Any modification made to `s_ref` will be reflected in `s`, and vice-versa, because they are simply alternative names for the same object.

## 2.5  Classes

Classes are the most significant new feature in C++. Classes are similar to C structures, except that they provide three additional capabilities: protection, member functions, and inheritance.

We need to talk about three people in discussing classes: the author or designer, who writes the class; the user, who uses the class in unmodified form as a tool in constructing their software, and the library designer, who may wish to use the functionality of an existing class as the basis for a new class.

It is frequently desirable in object-oriented programming to be sure that an object is internally consistent. This is not easy to accomplish in C because as the class designer you are dependent on the user to cooperate with you. There is no way to hide the details of the implementation from the user so that they can only use what you want them to use. This has two consequences. First, it is easy for a user to unwittingly forget a step in modifying an object, leaving the object in an inconsistent state. Second, it is impossible for the designer to improve the object's implementation with time, because there is no way to know how changes will break existing code. To find out, all of the source codes in which the object is used would have to be examined.

What is needed is a way to guarantee consistency. The first step is to have control over what a user can modify. To this end, a C++ class can declare members to be *private*:

```
class SimpleString {
  private:
    char *_string;
    int _length;
} ;
```

When a user declares a `SimpleString` object, they cannot access or modify the `_length` or `_string` members.

Given the ability to protect the contents of an object, it is useful to be able to provide controlled access to them. This is accomplished through *member functions*. Member functions are associated with an object type, and are permitted to modify the members of the object whether or not they are private.

To permit users access to the contents of a `SimpleString`, we can add a `string()` member function:

```
class SimpleString {
    char *_string;
    int _length;
  public:
    const char *string();
} ;
```

`Private:` and `public:` qualifiers can be inserted before any member. The author can declare members in whatever order is convenient. Members of a class are assumed to be private until the author says otherwise, so in this example the `private:` keyword is redundant. The `_string` and `_length` members are still private, but the `string()` function is public, which means that it can be called by users as follows:

```
SimpleString str;
printf(str.string());
```

The implementation for the `string()` member function is:

```
const char *
SimpleString::string()
{
    return _string;
} ;
```

Placing the class name and a double-colon "::" before the function name indicates that it is the definition of a member function. Note that the member names of the class are visible to member functions without any special syntax.

Because this member function returns a *constant* character pointer, a user cannot use the pointer to modify the contents of a `SimpleString`. It is occasionally useful to modify the contents of an object, so you might create another member function to permit this:

```
class SimpleString {
    char *_string;
    int _length;
  public:
    const char *string();
    void setString(const char *);
} ;
```

```
void
SimpleString::setString(const char *s)
{
    _string = new char[strlen(s)+1];
    strcpy(_string, s);
    _length = strlen(_string);
}
```

*user code:*

```
SimpleString str;
str.setString("fred");
```

## 2.6    Constant Member Functions

The introduction of member functions in classes leads to an interesting problem: if an object is declared `const`, how can C++ know which member functions can be called on that object? Because `SimpleString::string()` does not modify the contents of the object, it is legal for this operation to be performed on an object declared with the `const` keyword. A function that you can use safely on a constant object is a constant member function. By making a small change to this definition, you can let C++ know that this usage is legal:

```
class SimpleString {
    char *_string;
    int _length;
  public:
    const char *string() const;
    void setString(const char *);
} ;

const char *
SimpleString::string()
const
{
    return _string ? _string : "";
} ;
```

*user code:*

```
const SimpleString str = "fred";  // we'll get to this
str.setString("fred");    // illegal - nonconst member function
str.string();             // okay - const member function
```

It is an error for a constant member function to modify its object, and C++ will do its best to enforce this.

## 2.7   Operator Overloading

Calling member functions this way every time you wish to do something to a class object quickly makes the code difficult to read. Code written with the normal operators and syntax, such as:

```
a + b
```

is considerably easier to read than

```
a.add(b)
```

because it is more familiar. C++ provides the ability to enhance the language's built-in operators to understand new object types. This feature is called *operator overloading*. For example, it would be useful to be able to assign a string to the SimpleString. C++ permits you to define what assignment means in this context:

```
class SimpleString {
    char *_string;
    int _length;
  public:
    const char *string();
    void operator=(const char *);
} ;

void
SimpleString::operator=(const char *s)
{
    if (s) {
        _length = strlen(s);
        _string = new char[_length+1];
        strcpy(_string, s);
    }
    else {
        _length = 0;
        _string = 0;
    }
}
```

```
user code:

SimpeString str;
str = "fred";
```

C++ allows you to declare multiple versions of operators that have the same name but take different argument types. As far as C++ is concerned, overloaded operators are just like any other functions. The version of `SimpleString` shown does not permit you to assign one simplestring to another. The following version allows you to assign *either* a string or a `SimpleString` **to a** `SimpleString`:

```cpp
class SimpleString {
    // ...
  public:
    const char *string();
    void operator=(const char *);
    void operator=(const SimpleString&);
} ;

void
SimpleString::operator=(const char *s)
{
    delete _string;
    if (s) {
        _length = strlen(s);
        _string = new char[_length+1];
        strcpy(_string, s);
    }
    else {
        _length = 0;
        _string = 0;
    }
}

void
SimpleString::operator=(const SimpleString& s)
{
    delete _string;
    if (s._string) {
        _length = strlen(s._string);
        _string = new char[_length+1];
        strcpy(_string, s._string);
    }
    else {
        _length = 0;
        _string = 0;
    }
}
```

```
user code:

SimpeString str1, str2;
str1 = "fred";
str2 = str1;
```

Notice that the definition for `operator=` takes a `SimpleString` reference. This is to make sure that no temporary is created in the course of performing the assignment.

There is a problem with the definitions that we gave for `operator=`. Assignment in C is an operator: the result should be available as a value to code on the left of the assignment. You cannot, given these definitions, say

```
SimpleString s1, s2;
s1 = s2 = "fred";
```

because we have defined `operator=` to return `void`. C++ rewrites the code above as:

```
s1.operator=(s2.operator=("fred"))
```

and then complains that it doesn't know how to deal with:

```
s1.operator=(void)
```

It is incorrect to define `operator=` to return a `SimpleString`, because it creates a temporary in order to do so. The correct definition of `operator=` is:

```
class SimpleString {
    // ...
  public:
    const char *string();
    SimpleString& operator=(const char *);
    SimpleString& operator=(const SimpleString&);
} ;
```

```
SimpleString&
SimpleString::operator=(const char *s)
{
    delete _string;
    if (s) {
        _length = strlen(s);
        _string = new char[_length+1];
        strcpy(_string, s);
    }
    else {
        _length = 0;
        _string = 0;
    }
    return *this;
}

SimpleString&
SimpleString::operator=(const SimpleString& s)
{
    delete _string;
    if (s._string) {
        _length = strlen(s._string);
        _string = new char[_length+1];
        strcpy(_string, s._string);
    }
    else {
        _length = 0;
        _string = 0;
    }
    return *this;
}

user code:

SimpeString str1, str2;
str2 = str1 = "fred";
```

Returning a reference to *this means that the value visible from the assignment is the same as the left-hand side element in the assignment. This is a C++ reserved word. Within a member function, it refers to the current object. In binary operations, this is the object on the left-hand side of the operator.

Operator overloading is a very valuable and potentially very confusing feature. Use it in moderation.

## 2.8    Constructors

Making sure that an object remains internally consistent implies that it is necessary to be able to initialize objects properly when they are created. C++ supports this need through a mechanism called a constructor. A *constructor* is called whenever an object is declared or allocated in the heap.

The declaration

```
SimpleString s;
```

invokes the constructor with no arguments. If a class doesn't have any constructors, C++ builds one automatically. This is almost never the right thing to do. The solution is to provide a user-defined constructor to properly initialize the object. Constructors have no return value, and look like member functions whose name is the same as the class name:

```
class SimpleString {
    // ...
  public:
    SimpleString();
    // ...
} ;

SimpleString::SimpleString()
{
    _string = 0;
    _length = 0;
}
```

The constructor then initializes the _string member to be null, and the _length member to an appropriate value.

C++ distinguishes between assignment and initialization, which is sometimes a source of confusion.

```
SimpleString s1;            // Construction; no initialization
SimpleString s2 = "fred";   // initialization
// ...
s2 = "wilma";               // assignment; Not a declaration
```

Initialization is not the same as assignment. In order to have this initialization work correctly, an appropriate constructor must be defined:

```
class SimpleString {
    ...
  public:
    SimpleString(const char*);
    // ...
} ;

SimpleString::SimpleString(const char * s)
{
    if (s) {
        _length = strlen(s);
        _string = new char[_length+1];
        strcpy(_string, s);
    }
    else {
        _length = 0;
        _string = 0;
    }
}
```

There is one special constructor called the copy constructor:

```
SimpleString::SimpleString(SimpleString& s)
{
    if (s._string) {
        _length = strlen(s._string);
        _string = new char[_length+1];
        strcpy(_string, s._string);
    }
    else {
        _string = 0;
        _length = 0;
    }
}
```

The copy constructor is used to initialize one `SimpleString` from another, as in:

```
SimpleString s = "fred";
SimpleString s2 = s;    // uses copy constructor
```

If you do not define one, the C++ compiler will automatically generate one that does a memberwise copy of the elements. Historically this has been a buggy area of C++ compilers. The default constructor creation is primarily a way to provide backwards-compatible behavior for C structures.

## 2.9 Destructors

Each of the constructors has been carefully duplicating the string value by making a copy of it in the heap. When the object goes out of scope, it is useful to be able to make sure that this storage is reclaimed. The C++ destructor mechanism is used to make sure that the class designer gets an opportunity to clean up before the object goes away. The destructor is the member function whose name is the class name preceded by a "~":

```
class SimpleString {
    // ...
  public:
    ~SimpleString();
    // ...
} ;

SimpleString::~SimpleString()
{
    delete _string;
}
```

## 2.10 Inheritance

An important capability in object-oriented design is to be able to build on previous work. C++ provides a mechanism for specializing or changing the behavior of classes through inheritance. The original class is referred to as the base class. The enhanced or specialized version is referred to as the derived class or the subclass. An extended demonstration of how to use inheritance will be presented in the following section. There are two kinds of derivation: public and private. A publicly derived class is declared by saying:

```
class  DerivedClass : public BaseClass {
    // ... members needed by the new version ...
} ;
```

All of the public members of `BaseClass` will become public members of `DerivedClass`. Private members of `BaseClass` are not accessible from `DerivedClass`.

Sometimes it is useful to have members that are accessible to derived classes that are not accessible to the world at large. In addition to private and public, C++ has a third kind of visibility, *protected*, to describe such members. Protected members become protected members in a publicly derived class.

Classes can also be privately derived:

```
class  DerivedClass : private BaseClass {
    // ... members needed by the new version ...
} ;
```

All of the public members of `BaseClass` will become private members of `DerivedClass`. Protected members are visible in the immediately derived class, but are private in that class, so subsequent derivations will not see them.[2]

---

2    I have yet to see anyone make use of this capability in a real program.

## Exercises

1. Why is it important that call-by-reference is written the same way in the user's code as call-by-value?

2. The need for public and private visibility is fairly obvious. Why is protected needed? Is the end user of a class really different from the library designer who is trying to use existing work as a basis for a new class?

3. Early versions of C++ did not have a protected visibility class, so the default at the top of the class declaration is private. Now that protected has been introduced, should the default be changed? What kinds of things want to be hidden from library designers?

4. You should now know enough to implement `Slink`, a singly-linked list class. Do so.

5. Following the model of `Slink`, implement a class for doubly linked lists, `Dlink`.[3]

6. Now implement `Dlink` in C. How are the implementations different?

---

[3]  "Dlink" stands for Double Large Income, No Kids.

*I would like just once, just once, to be able to do the same thing again. Just once to try an evolutionary step instead of a confounded revolutionary one.*

*— H. Kinslow*

3

# An Extended Comparison

Linked lists are a convenient example for comparing C++ to C. Every programmer knows what they are and what they are supposed to do. Let's look at the problem of building a linked list of some structure, say, pieces of text. If you are interested in displaying them on a screen, then it is helpful for lines of text to have a length in addition to the actual string that makes up the line, so that you can handle wrap-around appropriately. In addition, you need a way to get to the next line of text.

## 3.1  `TextLine`: The C Version

By putting the requirements together, you might plausibly arrive at the following C structure:

```
typedef struct TextLine TextLine;

struct TextLine {
    TextLine  *next;   /* pointer to the next TextLine */
    char      *text;   /* pointer to the text itself */
    int       length;  /* length of the text */
} ;
```

There is more to defining lines of text than simply defining the structure that describes them. It is also necessary to define the operations that can be done on a line of text. There are two interrelated fields: the text body and the length of that body. There is nothing present in the data structure definition that ensures that these fields remain consistent. If you are

feeling properly paranoid, you would also provide a function to create
TextLine instances:

```
#include <malloc.h>
#include <string.h>

TextLine *
CreateTextLine(char *s)
{
    TextLine *tt = (TextLine *) malloc(sizeof(TextLine));
    if (!tt)
        FatalError("Out of memory\n");
    tt->next = 0;
    tt->text = s;
    tt->length = strlen(s);
    return tt;
}
```

You have now gone as far, in terms of specification, as C can take you.
More functions, such as TextLineAppend or TextLineRemove, could be
added to the repetoir, but at some point it becomes painful to have to use
them. The application author is quickly tempted to "optimize" their code
by writing modifications to TextLine directly, and there is no way to
prevent them from doing so. As things stand, there are two problems with
TextLine objects.

First, you don't have any control over what a user does to the contents of
the TextLine once you have created it. It would be very easy for a user to
modify either the length or the text fields and forget to modify the other.
In a program of several thousand lines, it's almost inevitable, even if the
user has good intentions. Further, an opening has been left for a more
serious design issue: because TextLine doesn't make a private copy of the
string, it is possible for the user to delete or otherwise modify the original,
leading to situations that are unpredictable at best. Whether or not this is a
problem depends on your view of how expensive it is to allocate and
deallocate memory, and whether you really want to have multiple copies
of things proliferating. In short, as the designer of the TextLine object,
you don't have a lot of control over what is done with it.

Second, you have mixed two distinct concepts about TextLine. The first
has to do with what it is to be a TextLine — an object that has some text

and associated length.  The second is that `TextLine` objects are singly linked, a fact that conceptually has very little to do with the behavior of the rest of a `TextLine`.  It would be better if you could build a set of generic routines for maintaining all of your linked list structures.

Finally, there isn't any firm relationship between `CreateTextLine` and the `TextLine` data structure.  At some level, you are depending on the user of the `TextLine` to follow the "honor system" and create `TextLine` instances in the way you intended.  When you come back to the code 18 months from now, what is the likelihood that you will remember the name of the `TextLine` construction routine?

## 3.2    `TextLine`: **The C++ Version**

Suppose you built the same object in C++.  The first thing to do is to make `TextLine` into a class so that you can bundle with it all of the operations that you want the user to be able to perform.  This bundling of data structure and operational specification is how C++ describes the abstraction of a `TextLine`.  The declaration is:

```
class TextLine {
    char *_text;
    int  _length;
public:
    TextLine *next;

    TextLine(char *s);
    ~TextLine();
} ;
```

The constructor and destructor for `TextLine` need to be implemented:

```
#include <string.h>

TextLine::~TextLine()
{
    delete _text;
}
```

```
TextLine::TextLine(char *s)
{
    if (s) {
        _length = strlen(s);
        _text = new char[_length+1];
        strcpy(_text, s);
    }
    else {
        _length = 0;
        _text = 0;
    }
}
```

In this case, the constructor requires that a string be given as an argument. This means that `TextLine` instances must be declared with an initializing string:

```
TextLine t("some string");
```

A declaration without an initializing string, such as:

```
TextLine t;
```

is an error, because this definition lacks a constructor that takes no arguments. If you wish to change this, you could add an appropriate constructor, like the one for `SimpleString`.

```
#include <string.h>

TextLine::TextLine()
{
    _length = 0;
    _text = 0;
}
```

The class as it stands is a considerable improvement over the C version, but a couple of problems need to be resolved. There is no way to get at the contents of a `TextLine` instance once you have created it. This is probably undesirable. You need to be careful to make sure that when you return the pointer to the string, it is returned in a way that prevents the user from mucking with it. In addition, you might like to be able to make a copy of a `TextLine` by initializing it from another `TextLine`. Finally, it would be nice if the user could change the value of a `TextLine` once it has been created, and could assign one `TextLine` to another.

The expanded `TextLine` declaration is:

```
class TextLine {
    char *_text;
    int  _length;
public:
    TextLine *next;

    TextLine(char *s);
    TextLine(TextLine&);

    TextLine& operator=(TextLine&);
    TextLine& operator=(char *);

    operator const char *() const;
    ~TextLine();
} ;
```

The class has a new constructor, `TextLine::TextLine(TextLine&)`.
This constructor permits you to initialize one `TextLine` from another:

```
TextLine tl1 = "fred";
TextLine tl2 = tl1;
```

The new class also defines what it means to assign one `TextLine` to
another, or to assign a string to a `TextLine`:

```
tl1 = "fred";
tl2 = tl1;
```

The C++ compiler will provide a default assignment rule, but no class
definition should be without one in practice.

Finally, this version of the class provides a way to get at the character
string inside an instance of `TextLine`. This is done by means of the
`operator const char *()` member function, which defines how to cast
a `TextLine` into a `char *`. With this operator defined, the following
assignment is legal:

```
const char * s;
s = tl1;
```

The assignment operators and the copy constructor need to be
implemented:

```cpp
#include <string.h>

TextLine&
TextLine::operator=(char *s)
{
    if (_text)
        delete _text;
    if (s) {
        _length = strlen(s);
        _text = new char[_length+1];
        strcpy(_text, s);
    }
    else {
        _length = 0;
        _text = 0;
    }

    return *this;
}

TextLine&
TextLine::operator=(TextLine& t)
{
    if (_text)
        delete _text;
    if (t._text) {
        _length = strlen(t._text);
        _text = new char[_length+1];
        strcpy(_text, t._text);
    }
    else {
        _length = 0;
        _text = 0;
    }

    return *this;
}

TextLine::operator const char *()
const
{
    return _text ? _text : "";
}

TextLine::~TextLine()
{
    delete _text;
}
```

```
TextLine::TextLine(TextLine& t)
{
    if (_text)
        delete _text;

    if (t._text) {
        _length = strlen(t._text);
        _text = new char[_length+1];
        strcpy(_text, t._text);
    }
    else {
        _length = 0;
        _text = 0;
    }
}
```

## 3.3    `TextLine`: One Last Round

All of the problems that we listed about `TextLine` have been addressed, with one exception: The new version still doesn't separate the linked-list functionality from the functionality associated with `TextLine`. It would improve the class to isolate the description of what it is to be a linked list element and compose this with our notion of what it is to be a text item to create `TextLine`.

The implementation of a singly linked list element (`Slink`) is well known; it basically consists of a pointer. In C, the structure might be:

```
typedef struct Slink Slink;

struct Slink {
    Slink *next;
} ;
```

You can build a similar data structure in C++, and encapsulate with it all of the additional functionality that you want a singly linked list to have. In addition to the pointer member, you need a way to link `Slink` instances together. The C++ version of `Slink` might be:

```
class Slink {
    Slink *_next;
public:
    Slink() { }
    ~Slink() {}
    Slink(Slink& s)
        { _next = s._next; }
    Slink& operator=(Slink& s)
        {_next = s._next; return *this; }

    Slink *setNext(Slink *sptr)
        { _next = sptr; return sptr; }
    Slink *next() const
        { return _next; }
} ;
```

C++ allows function definitions to be placed directly into the class declaration. These definitions are inlined (if possible) into the locations where they are used. Often, this technique can be used to altogether eliminate the cost of calling simple member functions. Because the member functions are defined in the declaration, there is no further implementation to be done for slink. The class is complete and ready to roll.

The definition for singly linked lists can be used as the basis for the TextLine class:

```
class TextLine : public Slink {
    char *_text;
    int  _length;
public:
    TextLine(char *s);
    TextLine(TextLine&);

    TextLine& operator=(TextLine&);
    TextLine& operator=(char *);

    operator const char *() const;
    ~TextLine();
} ;
```

The :public Slink says that TextLine *inherits* all of the operations that Slink supports in addition to the ones that TextLine supplies for itself. This version of the class really does address all of the problems we listed.

So what have you accomplished, other than doing a lot more typing for basically the same result as you had in the first place?

First, you have created a tool that will be useful in the future: the `Slink` class. Second, you have created a definition that protects the class. There is no way that a user can modify the contents of a `TextLine` in a way that leaves it inconsistent. Finally, you have completely encapsulated the behavior of `TextLine` in one centralized place. In this particular example, it might be that this wasn't really called for, but it is very difficult to know what kinds of things will be reused in the future, and you'll see classes very similar to `TextLine` arising in later chapters.

## Exercises

1. Some functions are not inherited by derivation, so they need to be rewritten in the derived class. One of these is the assignment operator, `operator=()`. Write an assignment operator that allows you to assign one `TextLine` to another.

2. One of the questionable design choices in TextLine is to have it hold null pointers. The assignment operators, constructors, and the implementation of `operator const char *()` are all forced to check for this special case explicitly. Would it be a better choice to have the pointer point to a zero length string? Why or why not?

3. Suppose for some reason you wish to keep `TextLine` instances in a circularly linked list. What is the smallest number of new classes that you would need to do the job? How many would it take to do the job right? Which way would *you* do it?

4. Implement `CircularList`, a generic container class for circularly linked lists of things.

6. Your boss informs you that the list of `TextLine` instances needs to be doubly linked after all. How many lines of code in the `TextLine` class need to be modified to accomplish the change, using the `Dlink` class from the exercises in the previous chapter (what do you *mean* you didn't do them)? How many lines would need to be modified, inserted, or deleted in the original C version of `TextLine` on page 6 to accomplish the same thing? What is the likelihood that the modified version would work the first time in each case?

7. Why is the `_next` member of the `Slink` class private rather than public? Is this a good design choice? Why or why not? Should it be protected instead?

*No engineer or programmer, no programming tools, are going to help us, or help the software business, to make up for a lousy design.*

— *I. Sharp*

4

# Designing Classes

When you have a class such as `iostream` already at hand, deciding whether to use it is pretty straightforward. However, designing your own classes is somewhat more complicated, and a good design goes through several stages. This chapter provides an introduction to class design that is developed further in later chapters.

A class is a template for an object. It describes what the object knows how to do, what it contains, and how it relates to other objects. Classes can be used to model the behavior of real-world objects, to encapsulate a conceptual entity, or to provide a concrete representation of a useful abstraction. A good design does all of these.

Designing classes well is something that comes with practice. It is a step by step process:

1. Choose the abstraction that your class will model, and how that abstraction relates to the surrounding environment.
2. Design the abstract datatype for the object. Figure out what operations the objects need to perform, and how they will interact with other parts of the program.
3. Choose a representation for the object.
4. Combine this abstract datatype and the representation to form a class definition.

5.  Think about how your class might be specialized, and what parts of the class should be visible to the derived classes.

6.  Think about how to generalize your class.

7.  Redesign and reimplement the class accordingly.

You may need several iterations to get it right, but the time is usually well spent. When the logic is clear and the class does what it needs to do, you are done. Frequently you will find that the code is small as well.

## 4.1   Abstract Datatypes

Programming in C++ is about building abstract datatypes. An abstract datatype is a description of the interface that an object provides. Ideally, an abstract datatype says nothing about how the object itself is implemented, or what the relationship between the implementation and the interface is. The actual implementation of a type is called its representation. The representation describes the implementation of the object — the names and layout of its fields and member functions. The distinction between abstract datatypes and representations is the most essential concept in object-oriented programming.

The simplest way to understand the difference is to look at an example: rectangles.

### *Representing Rectangles*

A rectangle is defined by a lower-left corner and an upper-right corner. One way to define rectangle is:

```
struct Rectangle {
    int upper_x;
    int upper_y;
    int lower_x;
    int lower_y;
} ;
```

Along similar lines, a circle might be defined as:

```
struct Circle {
    int   center_x;
    int   center_y;
    float radius;
} ;
```

Both definitions are correct and both get the job done, but neither is very flexible. The reason is that these definitions don't tell us anything about what it means for an object to be a rectangle or a circle. Instead, they describe the representation of the objects. They tell us how rectangles and circles are organized in memory.

The problem with representations is that they tend to change. For a given problem, several representations might be equally good. The optimal representation depends on the particular problem. There usually is no *a priori* way to choose any one of these good representations over another. For example, consider some other representations of a rectangle:

```
struct Point {
    int x, y;
} ;

struct Rectangle {
    Point lowerLeft;
    int height;
    int width;
} ;

struct Rectangle {
    Point center;
    int height;
    int width;
} ;
```

```
struct Rectangle {
    Point upperRight;
    int height;
    int width;
} ;

struct Rectangle {
    Point upperRight;
    Point lowerLeft;
} ;
```

None of these representations is intrinsically better or worse than the original. Which one is right for your application depends on what operations you are performing most often on your rectangles. It might even be desirable to use different representations in different parts of the same program.

The problem with using these definitions comes when you are obliged for one reason or another to change them. Given a program that depends on the existence of a `height` member, it might be a lot of work to change the representation to the two point version (the last version illustrated) if that becomes advantageous. Every location where the `height` member is referenced would need to be rewritten.

### *Rectangle: The Abstract Datatype*

Let's look at an abstract datatype for `Rectangle`. A rectangle is an object that has four vertices: a height, a width, a center, and a perimeter. An abstract datatype for rectangle might be:

```
class Rectangle {
  public:
    int height();
    int width();
    Point lowerLeft();
    Point upperRight();
    Point center();
} ;
```

This version says very little about how a rectangle is implemented. It describes the interface that a `Rectangle` knows how to satisfy, or if you like, the questions that a `Rectangle` knows how to answer.

There are other operations that a `Rectangle` might wish to perform. It would be nice to be able to change the position of a `Rectangle`, so you might want to add a `moveTo()` interface:

```
class Rectangle {
  public:
    // members as before

    Rectangle& moveTo(Point&);
    Rectangle& moveTo(int dx, int dy);
} ;
```

An abstract datatype defines only the interface to an object. It says as little as possible about the implementation.

### Combining Representations and Abstract Datatypes

The power of C++ lies in its ability to combine an abstract datatype with a representation in such a way that the users of an object can only make use of the defined interface, leaving the representation open to change, modification, or wholesale replacement. The mechanism by which this is accomplished is the C++ *class*. Combining the abstract datatype for rectangle with a representation, we might get:

```
class Rectangle {
    Point _upperRight, _lowerLeft;
  public:
    int height();
    int width();
    Point lowerLeft();
    Point upperRight();
    Point center();
    Rectangle& moveTo(Point&);
    Rectangle& moveTo(int dx, int dy);
} ;
```

The `upperRight` and `lowerLeft` members are private, which means that they cannot be directly manipulated by clients of the `Rectangle` class. User code therefore cannot be written to depend on the specific implementation of `Rectangle`.

C++ permits us to define some other parts of the type's interface as well: what happens when an instance is created, how an instance is initialized, and what happens when it is destroyed.

### What's the Advantage?

Let's go back to the first representation of a rectangle and implement the `moveTo()` operation for it. Rectangles aren't very interesting if we can't move them around and resize them. Here is a definition for `Rectangle::moveTo()`:

```
Rectangle&
Rectangle::moveTo(int dx, int dy)
{
    upper_x += dx;
    lower_x += dx;
    upper_y += dy;
    lower_y += dy;
    return *this;
}
```

A subtle problem is proliferating into the code. What happens when we switch to a coordinate system based on floating point numbers instead of integers? Even with just this one function implemented for both objects, we would already need to change several places if we decided to change coordinate systems.

The solution is to make the parameter and return types more abstract by naming them:

```
typedef int Coord;

Rectangle&
Rectangle::moveTo(Coord dx, Coord dy)
{
    upper_x += dx;
    lower_x += dx;
    upper_y += dy;
    lower_y += dy;
    return *this;
}
```

With this definition, we can change the coordinate system without altering the implementation at all.

## 4.2   Accessors and Mutators

Before you think about specializations for Rectangle, it is worthwhile to know the terminology for some things you have already done. A C++ class definition defines its interface in terms of member functions. Member functions provide access to the underlying representation, both to examine it and to modify it.

Given an object representation, there are two ways that you can make a member available for use by clients: make it public or insert a member function that lets the user retrieve the value. Making a part of the representation public makes it part of the interface, which means that it cannot subsequently be changed. Which way you do this is partly a matter of taste. A good rule of thumb is: never make a data item public unless you absolutely have to.

The abstract datatype approach is to make use of member functions. At the cost of doing a little extra work, the member function approach lets the class designer retain much more control. Functions that provide access to object members in this way are called accessors.

Two major advantages to using accessors are:

- The underlying implementation can be changed without having to eliminate the ability to get at the value. Suppose, for example, we changed our representation of `Rectangle` to be based on a center point, a width, and a height. `LowerLeft` can still be provided if the interface went through a function.

- There is no way for the client to modify the actual representation unless we let them. A function can return a reference to the internal object if you want the client to be able to modify it. It can return a constant reference or an entirely new copy if you wish to prevent such modification.

Each of these advantages is significant. There are some disadvantages to accessors as well:

- There is more to type (specifically, an open and close parentheses).

- The interface doesn't look like C, and it takes some getting used to.

- A function result isn't assignable unless the function returns a reference.

  For example:

  ```
  myCircle.center() = Point(3,5);
  ```

  is a syntax error. There is a solution to this, which you'll see shortly.

Some programmers argue that access functions are more expensive than simply doing the corresponding member access, because the access function needs to be invoked.   The problem they wish to avoid is the overhead of performing the function call to access the field.   The C++ `inline` keyword can be used to make sure that most accessors and mutators cost no more than the corresponding member access:

```
class Rectangle {
    // ...
  public:
    inline const Point& lowerLeft()
      { return ll; }
    inline Point center()
      { return (ur + ll) / 2; }
} ;
```

Functions that are defined within the class definition are implicitly declared `inline`, so the `inline` keyword in this example is not strictly necessary.   The `inline` keyword would be needed if the function appeared outside of the class definition:

```
class Rectangle {
    // ...
  public:
    const Point& LowerLeft();
} ;

inline
const Point&
lowerLeft()   { return ll; }
```

### Mutators

The major problem with using access functions is assignment to a member.   What happens when you want a user to be able to modify a class member?   To manage assignment, you need to introduce another class of functions, mutators, so called because they mutate the contents of an object.   We have already seen an example of such a function: `Rectangle::moveTo()` is a mutator:

```
Rectangle::moveTo(Coord dx, Coord dy)
{
    upper_x += dx;
    lower_x += dx;
    upper_y += dy;
    lower_y += dy;
    return *this;
}
```

The advantages to using mutators are:

- The class designer retains complete control over what can be altered.

- The class designer has an opportunity to make sure that a change to one part of an object is consistent with the rest of the object.

- Making mutations explicit leads to uniformity of programming style, leading to ease of maintainance.

An object needs to have as many accessors as there are things we need to look at, and as many mutators as there are ways we might want to change it. Like accessors, mutators that simply change the value of an object can almost invariably be inlined, which minimizes any run-time overhead.

An implementation of `Rectangle` with accessors and mutators might be:

```
class Rectangle {
    Point _ll;
    Point _ur;

  public:
    Coord height();
    Coord width();

    Rectangle(const Point& p1, const Point& p2)
      { _ll = p1; _ur = p2; }

    Point lowerLeft()
      const { return _ll; }
    Point upperRight()
      const { return _ur; }

    Point center()
      const { return (_ur + _ll) / 2; }
```

```
      Rectangle& moveTo(Point&);
      Rectangle& moveTo(Coord dx, Coord dy);

      Rectangle& setWidth(Coord w)
         { _ur.setX(_ll.x() + w); return *this; }
      Rectangle& setHeight(Coord h)
         { _ur.setY(_ll.y() + h); return *this; }
};

Rectangle&
Rectangle::moveTo(Point& where)
{
    _ur += _ll - where;
    _ur += where;
    return *this;
}

Rectangle&
Rectangle::moveTo(Coord dx, Coord dy)
{
    _ll += Point(dx,dy);
    _ur += Point(dx,dy);
    return *this;
}
```

Notice that the _ll and _ur members have been made private, in keeping with the discussion of abstract datatypes.  You are free to change the representation at any time without affecting client programs.  The practical importance of this cannot be overemphasized.

### When to Go Public

The alternative to accessors and mutators is to make a class member public.  A data item should only be made public when it satisfies both of the following conditions:

- You don't care if the client modifies the item at arbitrary times in arbitrary ways.  There is no need for consistency between this data member and the other members of the class.  (This is like saying the data item is unrelated to the rest of the class, in which case we might wonder why it needs to be in the class at all.)

- The data item in question can not be generalized because it is intrinsically related to the specific class at hand.

Making members public is usually a mistake. The style of object-oriented programming is to think of objects as having operations that can be done on them rather than members that can be accessed.

## Exercises

1.  What other operations are commonly performed on rectangles? Add some of them to the `Rectangle` class.

2.  `Coord` doesn't fully solve the problem of divorcing us from an integer coordinate system.  It is still possible to design routines such as `perimeter()` that need to have a conditional return type that isn't a coordinate.  Propose a solution to this problem.

3.  If we decide to change over to using real as the implementation type for the coordinate system, how does the `Rectangle` class change?

4.  Suppose we decide that we need to move to a three-dimensional coordinate system.  How does the `Rectangle` class need to change?

5.  Many object-oriented languages, such as SmallTalk™ and Common Loops have no facility for creating private members.  Are private members important? Why?

*We must somehow or other form a*
*conceptual framework in which we can talk*
*about these things in a clean and*
*comprehensible way.*

— *C. Strachey*

5

# Inheritance

An existing class can be specialized by building a new class that is based
on the original but replaces or augments its interface. The new class
inherits from the old one. Inheritance is also used when two classes have
common functionality that can be captured by a new base class. This is
called factorization. Among other things, factorization can be used to
eliminate common code that is duplicated across a number of classes.

When you design a new class, it is worthwhile to think about how the class
might be adapted to form other classes. If you don't modify the class,
someone else may. Frequently such modifications reveal design flaws in
the original class that could be avoided by planning ahead. C++ provides
a language mechanism specifically to support adapting existing classes:
inheritance.

## 5.1   Specialization: The Square Class

Geometrically, a square is a special kind of rectangle; it is a rectangle
whose length and height are constrained to be the same. We can define
`Square` as:

```
class Square : public Rectangle {
  public:
    Square(const Point& p1, const Point& p2)
      : Rectangle(p1, Point(p2.x(), p2.x() - p1.x() + p1.x()))
      { }

    Square& moveTo(Point& p)
      { Rectangle::moveTo(p); return *this; }

    Square& setWidth(Coord w)
      { Rectangle::setWidth(w); Rectangle::setHeight(w);
        return *this; }

    Square& setHeight(Coord h)
      { Rectangle::setWidth(h); Rectangle::setHeight(h);
        return *this; }
} ;
```

`Square` inherits the `lowerLeft()`, `upperRight()`, and `center()` member functions from `Rectangle`. The definitions do not need to change because the existing ones will continue to do what you expect. It cannot inherit `Rectangle::moveTo()` because the inherited versions would return objects of type `Rectangle&`, not of type `Square&`. The `setHeight()` and `setWidth()` functions cannot be inherited either. The `Square` versions must maintain the constraint that all sides must have equal length.

Constructors are not inherited, so `Square` needs to provide its own. Notice that the `Square` constructor does not pay any attention to the height of the rectangle defined by the two points. This guarantees that one cannot construct a `Square` that is not in fact square. This can cause surprises if the user expects the `height` argument to be honored.

### Flaws in the Original Design

The constructor for `Square` reveals two design flaws in `Rectangle`. First, the constructor is awkward. It is not at all obvious what is being done in the initialization of the base class. The clarity of `Square` is also hampered by the fact that the `Square` class cannot see the _ll and _ur members of `Rectangle`, because they are private.

Access to _ll and _ur can be had by making them protected, which requires a one line change in the `Rectangle` class:

```
class Rectangle {
  protected:
    Point _ll;
    Point _ur;

  public:
    // ...members as before...
} ;
```

Protected members are visible to derived classes but act like private members to other users.

The constructor ugliness can be avoided by introducing a protected constructor in `Rectangle` that initializes the private members (in this case there are none), and leaves the initialization of the protected and public members to the derived class. Because this constructor is protected, it is only visible to derived classes, and cannot be called by user code:

```
class Rectangle {
  protected:
    Point _ll;
    Point _ur;

    Rectangle::Rectangle() {}

  public:
    // ...members as before...
} ;
```

The `Square` constructor could then be rewritten as:

```
class Square : public Rectangle {
  public:
    Square(const Point& p1, const Point& p2)
      : ()
      { int sidelen = p2.x() - p1.x();
        _ll = p1;
        _ur.setX(sidelen + _ll.x())
        _ur.setY(sidelen + _ll.y()); }
    // ...
} ;
```

This version of the constructor is no more efficient, but it may be more readable. Which one you prefer is largely a matter of taste. Bear in mind that for many base classes, proper initialization requires the use of temporary variables, in which case the private-only constructor is probably the better approach.

## 5.2    Factorization: The GeomObject Class

Another way that inheritance is used is to factor out functionality that is common to a number of classes. There are some operations that can be done on both rectangles and circles, or indeed on any geometric object. One example is the object intersection test:

```
intersects(GeomObject&)       tell if two objects intersect
```

`Intersects()` presents a problem though, because if there are $n$ different kinds of objects, you need $n^2$ different intersection routines. Testing for intersections between objects of types `Square`, `Circle`, and `Rectangle`, would require:

```
int Circle::intersects(Rectangle&)
int Circle::intersects(Circle&);
int Circle::intersects(Square&);
int Rectangle::intersects(Rectangle&)
int Rectangle::intersects(Circle&);
int Rectangle::intersects(Square&);
int Square::intersects(Rectangle&);
int Square::intersects(Circle&)
int Square::intersects(Square&);
```

What is needed is a common base type on which to do intersection tests:

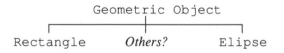

### Using a Common Base Class

The C++ inheritance mechanism is ideal for factoring out common functionality. You can create a generic geometric object and derive `Rectangle` and `Ellipse` from it. The generic object can hold the bounding box and can implement the `intersects()` operation:

```
class GeomObject {
  protected:
    struct {
      Point _ll, _ur;   // bounding box
    } _boundingBox;
  public:
    GeomObject(const Point& p1, const Point& p2)
      { _boundingBox._ll = p1; _boundingBox._ur = p2; }
    ~GeomObject()  {};

    Point center()     // return the center of the bounding box
      const
      { return (_boundingBox._ll + _boundingBox._ur) /2; }
    int intersects(const GeomObject& ob) const;
    int height()
      const { return _boundingBox._ur.y() -
                     _boundingBox._ll.y(); }
    int width()
      const { return _boundingBox._ur.x() -
                     _boundingBox._ll.x(); }
    const Point& upperRight()
      const { return _boundingBox._ur; }
    const Point& lowerLeft()
      const { return _boundingBox._ll; }

    GeomObject& moveTo(const Point& p)
      { _boundingBox._ur += (p - _boundingBox._ll);
        _boundingBox._ll = p; return *this; }

    GeomObject& operator=(const GeomObject& o)
      { _boundingBox._ur = o._boundingBox._ur;
        _boundingBox._ll = o._boundingBox._ll;
        return *this; }

    GeomObject& moveTo(const Point& delta)
      { _boundingBox._ll += delta;
        _boundingBox._ur += delta;
        return *this; }
};
```

## *Implementing the Bounding Box Test*

The idea behind the bounding box intersection test is to divide the coordinate space into regions around one object, and figure out which region contains the other object:

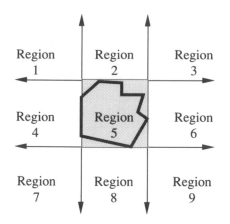

If no part of the second object lies in the shaded area (region 5), then it cannot intersect with the first. This can be checked by the following algorithm:

```
int
GeomObject::intersects(const GeomObject& o)
const
{
  if (upperRight().x() < o.lowerLeft().x() ||
      upperRight().y() < o.lowerLeft().y() ||
      lowerLeft().x() > o.upperRight().x() ||
      lowerLeft().y() > o.upperRight().y())
    return 0;
  return 1;
}
```

An excellent introduction to algorithms for computer graphics can be found in Foley and Van Dam's *Fundamentals of Interactive Computer Graphics.*

### A New Version of Rectangle

The new version of Rectangle is derived from the GeomObject class. Rectangle simply adds new member functions to the basic capabilities provided by GeomObject:

```
    class Rectangle : public GeomObject {
    public:
        Rectangle(const Point& p1, const Point& p2)
          : GeomObject(p1, p2)
          { }
        Rectangle(const Rectangle& r)
          : GeomObject(r.lowerLeft(), r.upperRight())
          { }
        Rectangle& operator=(const Rectangle& r)
          { GeomObject::operator=((GeomObject) r); return *this; }

        Rectangle& moveTo(const Point&);
        Rectangle& moveTo(Coord dx, Coord dy);
    } ;

    Rectangle&
    Rectangle::moveTo(Coord d, Coord dy)
    {
      GeomObject::moveTo(dx, dy);
      return *this;
    }
```

## 5.3   Virtual Functions

Frequently you will want to implement a common operation between two
classes whose implementation depends on the type of the object. It makes
sense to talk about moving geometric objects, but the implementation for a
`Circle` is very different from the implementation for a `Rectangle`. In
spite of this, it would be nice to be able to relocate an object without
knowing what kind it is. Virtual functions provide a way to do so. A
virtual function can be called from the base class, but the implementation
given in the base class can be replaced by the derived class. To make the
`moveTo()` function virtual, change its declaration in the `GeomObject` class
to:

```
    class GeomObject {
       // ...
      public:
       // ...
        virtual GeomObject& moveTo(Coord dx, Coord dy)
          { boundingBox._ll += delta;
            boundingBox._ur += delta;
            return *this;
          }
    }
```

The implementation shown will be used by any object type that doesn't supply its own version of `moveTo()`. Since `Rectangle` supplies a replacement, the `Rectangle` version will be used instead for all rectangles; even if the user only knows that they have a `GeomObject`. The Rectangle version of the move routine should also be declared `virtual`:

```
class Rectangle : public GeomObject {
    // ...
public:
    Rectangle(const Point& p1, const Point& p2)
      : GeomObject(p1, p2)
      { }
    Rectangle(const Rectangle& r)
      : GeomObject(r.lowerLeft(), r.upperRight())
      { }
    Rectangle& operator=(const Rectangle& r)
      { GeomObject::operator=((GeomObject) r); return *this; }

    virtual Rectangle& moveTo(const Point&);
    virtual Rectangle& moveTo(Coord dx, Coord dy);
} ;

virtual Rectangle&
Rectangle::moveTo(Coord dx, Coord dy)
{
  GeomObject::moveTo(Point(dx, dy));
  return *this;
}
```

## Exercises

1. As it turns out, the `Rectangle::moveTo()` function simply calls `GeomObject::moveTo()` and returns. Why isn't it good enough to simply eliminate `Rectangle::moveTo()` and let the version from `GeomObject` be visible?

2. Create a `Triangle` class using `Rectangle` as an example. How should the `moveTo()` function for such a class work?

3. `Polygon` should have a mechanism to add and delete vertices:

   ```
   Polygon::addVertBetween(const Point& v1,
                           const Point& v2,
                           const Point& newV)
   ```

   Implement this routine.

4. Similarly, `Polygon` needs a `deleteVertex()` routine. Implement one. What should happen when `deleteVertex()` is applied to a polygon that only has three vertices? What does your answer imply about well-designed classes?

5. `GeomObject::intersects()` errs on the side of conservatism, in that it sometimes claims that two objects intersect when they do not. This can be particularly irritating with triangles, as the bounding box covers at least twice the area of the triangle. It has the advantage that it is very cheap to implement. Propose an interface that would permit an object-specific intersection test to be applied when the two objects fall within the possibly intersecting region. Are there any cases for which your solution doesn't work?

6. If we were to introduce the ability to represent objects at arbitrary rotations, there are two systems we might use: rotating the object about its imaginary center point, or rotating it about some particular point. A third method that is cheaper than either of these is to rotate the object about the center of the bounding box. Argue the merits of each choice. Which would you use?

7. In which class(es) should the member describing the object's angle of rotation be implemented? Why?

8.  Rotation implies some substantial changes to bounding box maintainance. For each of the possible rotation methods described in problem 6, describe what additional information would need to be maintained in `GeomObject` to be able to keep the bounding box correct in the face of object rotation.

9.  Changing the actual stored values of the bounding box each time an object is rotated will, over time, introduce considerable rounding error in the bounding box boundaries. This is especially true if the boundaries are kept as integers, but it occurs with both single and double precision vertices as well. An alternative is to introduce a new class, `Rect`, which is simply the corners of a rectangle on the coordinate plane. We can then introduce

    ```
    const Rect GeomObject::boundingBox();
    ```

    and recompute the bounding box each time we need it, with no iterative loss of accuracy. Is this a good approach? Why or why not?

10. Introducing `Rect` is in fact the right solution. Suppose you already had a bunch of classes out there that expected to just look at the `boundingBox` member? Can anything be done to avoid rewriting them? What change to the original version of `GeomObject` would have protected us from needing to rewrite these classes? What does this imply about how to design objects?

## 6

*If I have any interest in computing science at all it is based on my firm belief that very often the most attractive solution is the most efficient one.*

*- E. Dijkstra*

# Putting It All Together

In chapter 4, the existence of a `Point` class was assumed, which did all of the things one would expect a point to do. This chapter describes how to build the `Point` class, putting together the material that has been covered in the first five chapters.

`Point` implements a geometric concept abstraction. A `Point` has an $x$ position and a $y$ position, both of which are of type `Coord`. An instance is created by supplying an initial $x$ and $y$ coordinate. You will want to be able to inquire about the current $x$ and $y$ values, and to be able to set them independently. The simplest version of `Point` that handles all of this is:

```
class Point {
    Coord _xpos, _ypos;
public:
    Point()
      { _xpos = 0; _ypos = 0; }
    Point(Coord x, Coord y)
      { _xpos = x; _ypos = y; }
    Point(const Point&);
    ~Point();

    Point& operator=(const Point&);
    Coord x()
      const { return _xpos; }
    Coord y()
      const { return _ypos; }
    void setX(Coord x)
      { _xpos = x; }
```

```
      void setY(Coord y)
         { _ypos = y; }
  } ;
```

The interface to this class provides access to all of the information that a user might need without exposing the implementation; the implementation can easily be changed, as we will see.

There are three functions that should be provided with every class definition: a default constructor, a copy constructor: X::X(X&), and an assignment operator. The default constructor is the one that takes no arguments:

```
Point::Point()
{
    _xpos = 0;
    _ypos = 0;
}
```

The copy constructor allows you to create a Point by initializing it from another Point:

```
Point::Point(const Point& other)
{
    _xpos = other.x();
    _ypos = other.y();
}
```

Assigning one Point to another is handled by:

```
Point&
Point::operator=(const Point& other)
{
    _xpos = other.x();
    _ypos = other.y();
    return *this;
}
```

Point is one of those rare classes for which a destructor isn't really needed. Even if none of the data items in the class need to be manipulated when an object is destroyed, an empty destructor should be provided. C++ uses it to make sure that destructors for member and base classes get called. Most class definitions also require a destructor, X::~X().

```
Point::~Point()   {}
```

The C++ compiler will try to provide a default copy constructor, assignment operator, and destructor if you don't give them in the class definition, but this is an area in which C++ compilers have traditionally had a lot of bugs. The best approach is to play it safe and supply your own versions of these functions.

## A Trick for Mutators

What should mutators return? There are a number of different traditions in various programming communities. One part of the LISP community recommends that a mutator should return the old value:

```
Coord
Point::setX(Coord newValue)
{
    Coord oldValue = _xpos;
    _xpos = newValue;
    return oldValue;
}
```

The other half of the LISP community says that mutators should return a copy of the *new* value:

```
Coord
Point::setX(Coord newValue)
{
    _xpos = newValue;
    return newValue;
}
```

The Scheme community is split down the middle, and since the language definition is done by consensus they decided to leave the return value of a mutator undefined, which means that different implementations do it different ways. From the standpoint of portable programming, this is equivalent to saying that the mutator returns nothing:

```
void
Point::setX(Coord newValue)
{
    _xpos = newValue;
}
```

This approach is about as cheap as the code can get and still mutate the object. The bad part is that the C convention of writing

```
a = b = 3;
```

doesn't work any more, and to do a sequence of mutations you are forced to write them out explicitly:

```
Point myPoint(4,6);

    // ...

myPoint.setX(5);
myPoint.setY(3);
```

Because of this, I prefer a fourth convention, which is to return a reference to the object that was modified:

```
Point&
Point::setX(Coord newValue)
{
    _xpos = newValue;
    return *this;
}
```

In addition to permitting the assignment syntax, this convention permits you to write:

```
myPoint.setX(5).setY(3);
```

The new versions of `Point::setX()` and `Point::setY()` are:

```
        Point& setX(Coord x)
          { _xpos = x; return *this; }
        Point& setY(Coord y)
          { _ypos = y; return *this; }
```

Return values and parameters are by far the two most common areas where the C++ reference feature is used. Returning a reference to an object is a particularly useful trick.

## 6.1 Point Arithmetic

The distance between two points (a vector) is something you need to be able to compute:

```
Point
Point::operator-(const Point& other)
const {
    return Point(_xpos - other.x(), _ypos - other.y());
}
```

You might argue that the return type of this function should be `Point`. Vectors and points, however, are essentially identical. Some geometry texts define points as vectors relative to the center of the coordinate system, and graphics transformations depend on the fact that this definition is correct. It would not be unreasonable to include a typedef:

```
typedef Point Vector;
```

This works because C++ considers the `Point` and `Vector` types to be the same.

Given a `Point`, you want to be able to add a vector to it:

```
Point
Point::operator+(const Point& vector)
const {
    return Point(_xpos + vector.x(), _ypos - vector.y());
}
```

Scaling a vector by the same amount in all directions is a useful thing to do:

```
Point
Point::operator*(Coord scale)
const {
    return Point(_xpos * scale, _ypos * scale);
}

Point
Point::operator/(Coord scale)
const {
    return Point(_xpos / scale, _ypos / scale);
}
```

With this definition, you can write:

```
rectangleCtr = (sq.upperRight() + sq.lowerLeft()) / 2;
```

## 6.2   Destructive Point Arithmetic

It would be nice to be able to do all of these operations destructively. Destructive operations are not legal on objects that have been declared to be constants, so they are not constant member functions. If you tried to make them constant member functions, the C++ compiler would (in theory) complain:

```
Point&
Point::operator-=(const Point& vector)
{
    _xpos -= vector.x();
    _ypos -= vector.y();
    return *this;
}

Point&
Point::operator+=(const Point& vector)
{
    _xpos += vector.x();
    _ypos += vector.y();
    return *this;
}

Point&
Point::operator*=(Coord scale)
{
    _xpos *= scale;
    _ypos *= scale;
    return *this;
}

Point&
Point::operator/=(Coord scale)
{
    _xpos /= scale;
    _ypos /= scale;
    return *this;
}
```

The `Point` class is finally complete. Folding all of these functions back into the class definition, you should arrive at the completed version:

```
class Point {
    int _xpos, _ypos;
public:
    Point();
    Point(Coord, Coord);
    Point(const Point&);
    ~Point();

    Point& operator=(const Point&);

    Point operator-(const Point&) const;
    Point operator+(const Point&) const;
    Point operator*(Coord) const;
    Point operator/(Coord) const;

    Point& operator-=(const Point&);
    Point& operator+=(const Point&);
    Point& operator*=(Coord);
    Point& operator/=(Coord);

    Coord x() const;
    Coord y() const;

    Point& setX(Coord);
    Point& setY(Coord);
} ;
```

The accessors and mutators are all public. As you can see, there is quite a bit to this class. In spite of the fact that there are a lot of member functions, this version of Point takes no more space in memory than the original.

## 6.3   Going 3-D

There is a fundamental problem with using Point as an example that you should be aware of. It can be illustrated by looking at what happens when you decide to go from two dimensions to three dimensions. The change to the definition of Point seems small:

```
class Point3d {
    int _xpos, _ypos, _zpos;
public:
    Point3d();
    Point3d(Coord, Coord, Coord);
    Point3d(const Point3d&);
    ~Point3d();
```

```
      Point3d operator-(const Point3d&) const;
      Point3d operator+(const Point3d&) const;
      Point3d operator*(Coord) const;
      Point3d operator/(Coord) const;

      Point3d& operator=(const Point3d&);
      Point3d& operator-=(const Point3d&);
      Point3d& operator+=(const Point3d&);
      Point3d& operator*=(Coord);
      Point3d& operator/=(Coord);

      Coord x() const;
      Coord y() const;
      Coord z() const;

      Point3d& setX(Coord);
      Point3d& setY(Coord);
      Point3d& setZ(Coord);
};
```

but it isn't. The impact of this change on client code is tremendous. All of the objects that were built around `Point` were designed with the assumption that they operated in a two dimensional coordinate system. Suddenly they have to live in three dimensions. To illustrate the problem, the old implementation of `intersects()` is simply broken:

```
GeomObject::intersects(GeomObject& o)
{
  if (upperRight().x() < o.lowerLeft().x() ||
      upperRight().y() < o.lowerLeft().y() ||
      lowerLeft().x() > o.upperRight().x() ||
      lowerLeft().y() > o.upperRight().y())
    return 0;
  return 1;
}
```

The move from two dimensions to three is more than a change of implementation. It is a fundamental shift in paradigm. At the very least, the new class should be renamed to avoid breaking existing code. Calling it `Point3d` gives users an indication that the new class is related to the old one while making it clear that the new version is substantially different.

## Exercises

1. The _xpos and _ypos members of the `Point` class are private. Why isn't it necessary for them to be protected?

2. The problem with `Point3` is that we want to be able to mix modes. Just because there is a third dimension doesn't mean that all of our objects need to live in it. Give an assignment operator that lets us assign a `Point` to a `Point3`. Give a rationale that explains why the assignment's implementation makes sense.

3. We have seen that the problem of going from two dimensions to three dimensions is a fundamental move. What about adding a fourth dimension?

4. Returning a reference to the modified object can lead to surprises. What mutators should not return a reference?

5. Define a variation on `Rectangle` that works in three dimensions. Compare it to the two dimensional rectangle class. Can you define an assignment operator that lets the user assign a two-dimensional rectangle to a three-dimensional one?

6. What about assigning a three-dimensional rectangle to a two-dimensional rectangle? See if you can figure out how to do this without modifying the `Rectangle` class.

*Since we have finite skulls, we have to have reasonably concise representations.*
— *A. Falkoff*

7

# Bit Sets

Implementing bit sets in C is an ugly problem. Bit sets are typically represented as an array of unsigned longs and a collection of macros. The need for macros is unfortunate because they don't behave like functions and can lead to disconcerting surprises. In addition, implementing bit sets as arrays means that they are not first-class objects. They cannot be passed by value and they cannot be returned by functions. To make this clear, consider the following implementation for a bit set large enough to cover the 8-bit ASCII character set:

```
typedef unsigned long Set256[8];
Set256 CharSet;
// ...
CallAFunctionWith(CharSet);
```

Because `Set256` is implemented as an array, no copy of the set is made. It is passed by reference, in keeping with C (and C++) rules. This isn't obvious to the user because `Set256` looks like any other type name. From the user's perspective, this is a bug.

A better solution would be to use a structure:

```
struct Set256 {
    unsigned long bits[8];
};
```

With minor alterations to the macros, this version is just as easy to manipulate, but can be passed by value or returned from a function.

Stylistically, the declaration still leaves something to be desired. It assumes that an unsigned long is 32 bits, which isn't true on all machines. A better declaration might be:

```
typedef unsigned long Set256[256/(sizeof(unsigned long) * 8)];
```

This version is no less efficient and it will work on any machine that has 8 bit bytes.

## 7.1   Bit Sets in Abstract

What operations should bit sets be able to do? The obvious operations for setting and clearing members of the set are:

| | |
|---|---|
| *clear* | Turns off all of the items in a bit set. |
| *fill* | Turns on all of the items in a bit set. |
| *add* | Adds a single member to a bit set. |
| *remove* | Removes a single member from a bit set. |

Bit sets should also implement the traditional set operations between two sets *A* and *B*:

| | |
|---|---|
| *union* | Turn on all items in either *A* or *B*. |
| *intersection* | Turn on all items in both *A* and *B*. |
| *difference* | Turn on items in *A* not in *B*. |
| *exclusive-or* | Turn on items in *A* or *B* but not in both. |

Finally, bit sets should support assignment and comparison. For performance reasons, it should be possible to do most of the operations destructively.

What about operations between bit sets of different sizes? You might consider doing an intersection of a set of 8 bits with a set of 32 bits. For this chapter, let's ignore this issue, though defining a sound mathematical system of what such operations should mean is an interesting problem. The implementation of bit sets presented here is not general. Our operations will work only on sets that are the same size.

On the UNIX system and many others, some system calls expect to be passed a bit set. Some examples from include the *select* and *poll* system calls. In order to simplify working with these system functions, it is useful for the address of a BitSet object and the address of the actual array of bits be the same. By doing so, it becomes possible to write:

```
result = poll(&set1, set1.size(), 0);
```

An implication of this is that bit sets cannot have any virtual members because there is no way that you can control where the virtual table pointer will appear in the representation. In most current C++ implementations, it is the first element of the structure, which in this case would be a very bad thing indeed.

## 7.2   The Basic Implementation

The Set256 class could be defined as:

```
class Set256 {
    unsigned long bits[256/(sizeof(unsigned long) * 8)];
public:
    Set256()
        { memset(bits, 0, sizeof(bits)); }
    ~Set256()
        { }

    Set256& clear()
        { memset(bits, 0, sizeof(bits)); }
    Set256& fill()
        { memset(bits, ~0, sizeof(bits)); }

    // assignment and initialization:
    Set256(Set256& s);
    Set256& operator=(Set256& s);

    // operations on elements:
    Set256 operator &(unsigned u);
    Set256 operator |(unsigned u);
    Set256 operator -(unsigned u);
```

```
    // destructive versions:
    Set256& operator &=(unsigned u);
    Set256& operator |=(unsigned u);
    Set256& operator -=(unsigned u);

    // operations on Set256s:
    Set256 operator &(Set256& s);
    Set256 operator |(Set256& s);
    Set256 operator -(Set256& s);

    // destructive versions:
    Set256& operator &=(Set256& s);
    Set256& operator |=(Set256& s);
    Set256& operator -=(Set256& s);
} ;
```

Here are sample implementations of each kind of operator. The others are implemented similarly:

```
#define ULONG_BITS (sizeof(long) * 8)

Set256&
Set256::operator &=(unsigned u)
{
    bits[u/32] &= (u+1) % 32;
    return *this;
}

Set256
Set256::operator &(unsigned u)
{
    Set256 newSet(*this);

    newSet &= u;
    return newSet;
}

Set256&
Set256::operator &=(Set256& b)
{
    int i;
    for(i = 0; i <= 256/ULONG_BITS; i++)
        bits[i] &= b.bits[i];
    return *this;
}
```

```
Set256
Set256::operator &(Set256& b)
{
    Set256 newSet(*this);

    newSet &= b;
    return newSet;
}
```

The balance of the class implementation should be straightforward.

## 7.3 Generic Bit Sets

The set256 class serves its purpose adequately, but it would be better to have a way to specify the size of a BitSet in a more generic way. Using macros, you can build a mechanism to do this:

```
#ifndef ULONG_BITS
#define ULONG_BITS (sizeof(unsigned long)*8)
#endif

#define MakeBitSet(size)                                    \
class name2(BitSet,size) {                                  \
    unsigned long bits[size/ULONG_BITS];                    \
public:                                                     \
    name2(BitSet,size)()                                    \
        { memset(bits, 0, sizeof(bits)); }                  \
    name2(BitSet,size)()                                    \
        { }                                                 \
    /* ... rest of BitSet members ... */                   \
} ;
```

The use of name2() deserves explanation. Name2 is a macro that is defined in the generic.h header file. Generic.h should be part of your C++ distribution. What the macro does is to splice together its arguments to form a single identifier. A use of the macro, as in

```
name2(Two, Parts)
```

is converted by the preprocessor into the single token

```
TwoParts
```

The name2() macro is used throughout *A C++ Toolkit* to generate names for generic classes. There is a proposal to add a new language feature called "templates" that would allow us to build generic classes within the language.   The templates proposal has not yet been adopted or implemented.   It isn't likely that the templates mechanism will be available any time soon.   The templates proposal is discussed in greater detail in a later chapter.

This version has a bug, however.   Look at what happens when you write

```
MakeBitSet(8);
```

The macro expands into

```
class BitSet8 {                                                       \
    unsigned long bits[8/32];                                         \
public:                                                               \
    /* ... rest of BitSet members ... */                             \
} ;
```

Because of the rules for integer division, 8/32 becomes 0, so the declaration turns into:

```
class BitSet8 {                                                       \
    unsigned long bits[8/32];                                         \
public:                                                               \
    /* ... rest of BitSet members ... */                             \
} ;
```

C++ does not permit arrays with zero elements.   A slightly more clever algorithm for computing the array size addresses this issue:

```
#ifndef ULONG_BITS
#define ULONG_BITS (sizeof(unsigned long)*8)
#define ULONG_SHIFT 4    /* assumes 32 bit long */
#endif

#define MakeBitSet(size)                                              \
class name2(BitSet,size) {                                            \
    unsigned long bits[(size+ULONG_BITS)>>ULONG_SHIFT];              \
public:                                                               \
    name2(BitSet,size)()                                              \
        { memset(bits, 0, sizeof(bits)); }                          \
    name2(BitSet,size)()                                              \
        { }                                                          \
    /* ... rest of BitSet members ... */                             \
} ;
```

This version guarantees that sets whose size is not a multiple of ULONG_BITS will work correctly.

The implementation also needs to be turned into a macro. The definitions for the Bitset::clear() and Bitset::fill() functions are straightforward:

```
#define MakeBitSet(size)                                          \
class name2(BitSet,size) {                                        \
    unsigned long bits[(size+ULONG_BITS)>>ULONG_SHIFT];          \
public:                                                           \
    // ...                                                        \
    name2(BitSet,size)& clear()                                   \
        { memset(bits, 0, sizeof(bits));                          \
            return *this; }                                       \
    name2(BitSet,size)& clear()                                   \
        { memset(bits, ~((unsigned long)0), sizeof(bits));  \
            return *this; }                                       \
    /* ... rest of BitSet members ... */                         \
} ;
```

The other operators follow the pattern:

```
#define MakeBitSet(size)                                          \
class name2(BitSet,size) {                                        \
    unsigned long bits[(size+ULONG_BITS)>>ULONG_SHIFT];          \
public:                                                           \
    // ...                                                        \
    name2(BitSet,size)& operator &=(unsigned u)                   \
        { bits[u/32] &= (u+1) % 32;                               \
            return *this; }                                       \
    name2(BitSet,size)& operator +=(unsigned u)                   \
        { bits[u/32] |= (u+1) % 32;                               \
            return *this; }                                       \
    name2(BitSet,size)& operator |=(unsigned u)                   \
        { bits[u/32] |= (u+1) % 32;                               \
            return *this; }                                       \
    name2(BitSet,size)& operator -=(unsigned u)                   \
        { bits[u/32] &= ~((u+1) % 32);                            \
            return *this; }                                       \
    /* ... rest of BitSet members ... */                         \
} ;
```

Including both BitSet::operator+=() and BitSet:::operator|=() imposes no extra size, and permits users to interchangeably use either of the natural ways to say "add a member to this set."

## 7.4   Coping with Compiler Brain Death

To date, most of the existing C++ compilers do not know how to inline functions containing loops or gotos. As a result, the implementation of the set operations as shown probably isn't the best one in practice. If you are concerned with portability and code size, the looping procedures should be taken out of line.

Because most C++ systems are based on the AT&T *cfront* translator, it is useful to understand the strategy that *cfront* uses when it is unable to inline a function. When a function is declared `inline`, the translator must decide what to do with it. If it is able to inline the function, all is well. If it can't, a problem arises. The function was defined in a header file that might be included by hundreds of source files. If it were written out in every source file, a large amount of space would be wasted.

The translator does everything it can to avoid this possibility. If the class has any member functions that are *not* inline, C++ makes a note of the first of them. When it sees the implementation of this function in a source file, it writes the inlined function in that source file as well. This heuristic is certainly better than nothing, and is the same one used to decide where to implement virtual functions.

Sometimes there is no such member function. In this case, the C++ compiler makes a copy of the inline function in every file that uses the function. In order to ensure that two such functions do not conflict, all are wriiten out as `static` functions. One of the versions of *cfront* that I used to test the examples in this book has been "enhanced" to consider this an error rather than a warning.

Avoiding the inlining problem seems to be the safest path. Fortunately, it is possible to cope with the problem portably by using the preprocessor:

```
#ifdef BRAINDEAD_INLINER
extern void memor(unsigned long *, unsigned long *, int);
extern void memand(unsigned long *, unsigned long *, int);
extern void memsub(unsigned long *, unsigned long *, int);
#else
inline
void memor(unsigned long *s1, unsigned long *s2, int len)
{  for(int i = 0; i < len; i++) s1[i] |= s2[i];  }
inline
void memand(unsigned long *s1, unsigned long *s2, int len)
{  for(int i = 0; i < len; i++) s1[i] &= s2[i];  }
inline
void memsub(unsigned long *s1, unsigned long *s2, int len)
{  for(int i = 0; i < len; i++) s1[i] -= s2[i];  }
#endif
```

These functions can be implemented by a library and used in the inline members of the class:

```
#define MakeBitSet(size)                                        \
class name2(BitSet,size) {                                      \
    unsigned long bits[(size+ULONG_BITS)>>ULONG_SHIFT];         \
public:                                                         \
    // ...                                                      \
    name2(BitSet,size)& operator +=(name2(BitSet,size)& b)      \
        { memor(bits, b.bits, size/ULONG_BITS);                 \
          return *this; }                                       \
    name2(BitSet,size)& operator *=(name2(BitSet,size)& b)      \
        { memand(bits, b.bits, size/ULONG_BITS);                \
          return *this; }                                       \
    name2(BitSet,size)& operator -=(name2(BitSet,size)& b)      \
        { memsub(bits, b.bits, size/ULONG_BITS);                \
          return *this; }                                       \
    name2(BitSet,size)& operator |=(name2(BitSet,size)& b)      \
        { memor(bits, b.bits, size/ULONG_BITS);                 \
          return *this; }                                       \
    /* ... rest of BitSet members ... */                       \
} ;
```

Note that they are not member functions, which lets us avoid having to define an ImplementBitSet macro.

A case could be made that a better solution is not to inline these troublesome routines in the first place. Unfortunately, set operations have a way of appearing in inner loops, and inlining the functions is essential if an optimizer is to be expected to do a good job with these computations.

## Exercises

1.  As this chapter mentions, the bit set implementation could be generalized to do operations on sets of different sizes, provided that the entries in the two bit sets are zero relative. Give a definition of what each of the operations mean on bit sets of unlike size.

2.  Implement the assignment operator and copy constructor for the generic `BitSet`. Test your results.

3.  The macro versions of the `BitSet` class could be simplified by defining a second macro

    ```
    #define BitSet(size) name2(BitSet,size)
    ```

    This form has the advantage that it is much closer to the templates proposal than the version used in this chapter. Rewrite part of the generic `BitSet` class to use this form and see which one is easier to follow.

4.  How should this class be documented so that it is clear how it should be used?

5.  Why is it so difficult to write an compiler that does effective inlining while generating C code?

6.  All of the members of the `BitSet` class are inline. Some of them are used infrequently enough that they shouldn't be. Decide which ones and construct the appropriate `ImplementBitSet` macro.

*The difficulty with obscure bugs is that the probability of their appearance increases with time and with wider use.*

*— J. Reynolds*

# 8

# Lists

Computer science has the interesting property that the vast majority of problems are solved with a very small number of fundamental data structures. These data structures are used so often that they have achieved the status of koans. The most common by far is the linked list. If you have been programming for more than a year or two, you can probably write them in your sleep. Initially, I thought linked lists were too basic a topic for this book. A recent project changed my mind.

I found myself working on a project that needed linked lists in several places. Having written several hundred linked list data structures in my career, I threw one together without bothering to build a class. No sooner had I completed the first list than I needed to build a second, and cranked out the code for that one, too. Does this sound familiar? Alarm bells went off in my head and I decided that this chapter was worth including.

When I began to think about how to present lists, I realized that they were well worth investigating in this book. List data structures raise at least one interesting engineering issue, and expose one of the ways in which the strong typing features of C++ can hurt rather than help.

## 8.1   List Basics

The traditional *Data Structures* course has a host of terms for every variety of list one might desire to contemplate (personally I prefer to contemplate other things).  Singly-linked lists, doubly-linked lists, stacks, queues, hashed queues, and so on, are simply different applications of the same basic data structure.

I have always found it surprising that the textbooks work so hard to differentiate these fundamentally similar data structures.  In writing this book, I went back over the more common data structures texts and tried to figure out why they make the topic so complicated.  The problem with the traditional descriptions of these data structures is that they fail to separate the implementation from the policy.  Focusing on the implementation means making the implementation useful to as many kinds of users as possible.  Focusing on the policy means facilitating only "right thinking" uses of the abstraction.  It is sometimes necessary to establish policy with an implementation.  Usually, setting a policy just limits the utility of the tool.

### *List Elements*

The basic part of a list is the list element.  Traditional descriptions of list elements give a structure that looks something like:

```
struct Link {
    Link *next;
    Link *prev;
    void *listItem;
};
```

The idea is that the linked item itself is not a part of the list, but is pointed to by the list element:

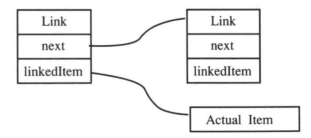

In practice, real implementations simply make the `next` and `prev` pointers be a part of the list element to avoid the extra pointer indirection.  The disadvantage to this approach is that it becomes impossible to manipulate the lists generically. To swap the ordering of two elements in the list you shouldn't really have to care what the actual items are.

In C++, you can get the best of both of these worlds by making the link data structure be a base class:

```
class Link {
    friend class List;
 protected:
    Link *_next;
    Link *_prev;
 public:
    Link()
        { _next = _prev = 0; }
    virtual ~Link();
    Link *next()
        { return _next; }
    Link *prev()
        { return _prev; }
} ;
```

Notice that links do not know how to insert themselves into a list! This lets the same underlying data structure be used to handle FIFO lists (queues), and LIFO lists (stacks). Conversely, while links know how to disentangle themselves from each other, they make no attempt to keep the overall list up to date. The policy of how items are inserted and removed is separated from the implementation of the list elements.

A correct application will not delete a list element before deleting the element from its parent list. Consequently, the destructor is written as:

```
Link::~Link()
{
    if (_next) _next->_prev = _prev;
    if (_prev) _prev->_next = _next;
    _next = 0;
    _prev = 0;
}
```

### The List Head

Having implemented the `Link` class, you now need to implement the class that describes the list as a whole. In a traditional data structures course, this is called the list head:

```
class List {
 protected:
    Link * first;
    Link *_last;
 public:
    List()
        { _first = _last = 0; }
    virtual ~List();
    Link *last()
        { return _last; }
    Link *first()
        { return _first; }

    List& append(Link *);
    List& prepend(Link *);
    List& remove(Link *);
} ;
```

The insertion management is implemented by the `List::append()` and `List::prepend()` member functions:

```
List&
List::append(Link *l)
{
    if (_last) {
        _last->_next = l;
        l->_prev = _last;
    }
    else
        _first = l;

    _last = l;

    return *this;
}
```

```
List&
List::prepend(Link *l)
{
    if (_first) {
        _first->_prev = l;
        l->_next = _first;
    }
    else
        _last = l;

    _first = l;

    return *this;
}
```

`List::remove()` simply ensures that the elements have no further ties to the list and the notions of the first and last elements are correctly maintained:

```
List&
List::remove(Link *l)
{
    if (l == _first)
        _first = _first->_next;
    if (l == _last)
        _last = _last->_prev;

    if (l->_next) {
        l->_next->_prev = l->_prev;
        l->_next = 0;
    }
    if (l->_prev) {
        l->_prev->_next = l->_next;
        l->_prev = 0;
    }

    return *this;
}
```

A queue is a list that operates in first-in first-out (FIFO) order. A stack operates in last-in, first-out (LIFO) order. A bit of thought should convince you that there is another way to think of this behavior:

- When you add an object to a stack, you want it to be the next object returned from the stack.

- When you add an object to a queue, you want it to be the last object returned from the queue.

This suggests that there isn't a compelling reason to think of queues and stacks as being different. Both lists start off empty. Both lists can be implemented on the `Link` and `List` classes shown above.

Users who prefer more traditional names for the stack operations may feel more comfortable if some trivial member functions are added:

```
class List {
 public:
    // ...
    List& push(Link *l)
        { return append(l); }
    Link *pop()
        { Link *l = _last;
          remove(_last);
          return l; }
    Link *top()
        { return _last; }
} ;
```

While purists might suggest that these functions belong in a `Stack` class, I am inclined to disagree. Including these members doesn't compromise the integrity of the `List` class in any way. Given this, multiplying classes seems unwarranted.

## 8.2    The Problem of Type Checking

The `List` classes have an awkward flaw. They necessarily compromise the type checking of C++. To see why this is so, let's look at a typical example of how the class gets used. Suppose we have some class that needs to live on a list:

```
class Object : public Link {
    // ...
} ;
```

Given such a class, you might want to iterate over a list of them, doing something to each:

```
{
    Object *o = (Object *) ListOfObjects.first();
    while (o) {
        DoSomethingTo(o);
        o = (Object *) o->next();
    }
}
```

The problem is that the return type of the `Link::next()` and `List::next()` member functions isn't what you want; it returns a pointer to a `Link` rather than a pointer to an `Object`. It was this problem that led me not to bother to build a class to do the various linked lists in my project originally. I was being unduly pessimistic. A macro solves the problem of building a `Link` class that type-checks in the right ways without the need for casts:

```
#define MakeLink(TYPE)                                        \
                                                             \
class name2(TYPE,Link) : public Link {                       \
 public:                                                     \
    name2(TYPE,Link)()                                       \
        : Link()                                             \
        { }                                                  \
    virtual ~name2(TYPE,Link)()                              \
        { }                                                  \
    TYPE *next()                                             \
        { return (TYPE *) _next; }                           \
    TYPE *prev()                                             \
        { return (TYPE *) _prev; }                           \
} ;
```

The casts throughout the code can now be avoided by writing:

```
class Object;
MakeLink(Object);

class Object : public ObjectLink {
    // ... contents of Object...
} ;
```

The `ObjectLink::next()` member returns the correct type and hides the version in the base `Link` class.

Similarly, a macro can be built to construct a properly type-checked `List` class.

```
#define MakeList(TYPE)                                            \
                                                                 \
class name2(TYPE,List) : public List {                           \
 public:                                                         \
    name2(TYPE,List)()                                           \
        : List()                                                 \
        { }                                                      \
    virtual ~name2(TYPE,List)()                                  \
        { }                                                      \
    TYPE *last()                                                 \
        { return (TYPE *) _last; }                               \
    TYPE *first()                                                \
        { return (TYPE *) _first; }                              \
                                                                 \
    TYPE *pop()                                                  \
        { return (TYPE *) List::pop(); }                         \
    TYPE *top()                                                  \
        { return (TYPE *) _last; }                               \
} ;
```

A type-safe list of objects can now be declared by writing:

```
class Object;
MakeLink(Object);
MakeList(Object);
```

## 8.3   An Implementation Note About Virtual Functions

An unfortunate consequence of the implementation of most C++ compilers is that they do not handle virtual functions correctly. Every C++ implementation to date implements virtual functions by emitting something called a virtual table. Because current linkers cannot be counted on to properly merge the virtual tables, various tricks are used to decide when to emit the virtual table, in the hope of emitting it only once.

Unfortunately, if a class has virtual functions but does not have any non-inline member functions, all of these tricks fail. Under these conditions, the C++ compiler is likely to emit virtual tables in every object module that is built. Even if the virtual table is only a few words, having several identical copies appear in several files can quickly consume significant amounts of data space.

My own way of avoiding this problem is that I never make the destructor an inline function. If there is at least one function that is not inlined, most of the compilers will emit the virtual table only in the source file where that function is defined.

If having the destructor be inlined is important (it can be if you are allocating and deallocating things rapidly and have defined your own delete operator), a workaround is to create a private non-inline function with a suitably obvious name, and implement it in a source file. It is probably cheaper to spend 20 bytes or so of code space than 20 Kbytes or so of data space if that is what it takes to eliminate the extra virtual tables.

Hopefully, linkers and compilers will soon improve to the point where this sort of trickery is no longer necessary.

## Exercises

1.  Designing the `Link` structure so that it has no knowledge of the list type is a debatable choice. What alternatives are there? Give some advantages and disadvantages for each.

2.  Define an assignment operator that copies one linked list to another. What should the semantics of this operation be? If the individual elements are to be copied, propose a mechanism for doing this.

3.  The macro solution for building generic classes isn't very pleasant, to say the least. See if you can come up with a better mechanism.

4.  `Link` is an implementation of a doubly linked list class. Sometimes a singly linked list would be good enough. Is it worth defining a different class to implement singly linked lists? Could the same interface be used in `SingleList` as in `DoubleList`? Is the result as robust?

5.  Now that you've defined the singly linked version, could you switch back and forth between the two painlessly? If not, is there a fundamental aspect of the abstraction that is different between the two lists or is your abstraction inadequately thought out?

6.  Is saving the extra word of memory per object a sufficient reason for implementing a singly linked list class?

7.  What would be required of a compiler system to solve the problem of multiple copies of virtual functions?

*Confession is good for the soul.*
                        — *R. McClure*

*. . . but bad for your career.*
                        — *A. d'Agapeyeff*

# 9

# Arrays

One of the aspects of C that is confusing to some newcomers is the handling of arrays. On the one hand, there are those who feel that arrays should provide bounds checking. On the other hand, there are those who feel a need for the dynamically sized arrays of BASIC. Both views have their merits, and ideally a language can provide both solutions. C++ provides the facilities needed to construct both styles of arrays.

## 9.1  An Array Class

If you are going to build a class that masquerades as a built-in object, it is important to bear in mind that the solution that causes the fewest surprises is usually the best one. This is known as the "Principle of Least Amazement." The result should look to the greatest extent possible like the built-in language feature. Doing things that appear straightforward should be straightforward. Finally, any extensions should operate in a way that is consistent with the way the built-in arrays operate.

The first step is to create a class that looks and feels to the programmer just like a C++ array, and then think about how to enhance it. The services that an array of type `T` provides are:

- Declaration of the size of the array.

- `Operator[]`, which provides for member access.

- Using the array name alone, which acts like a pointer to the first element.

- Initialization if the array is static or is declared at file scope.

The first three of these items seem straightforward enough to do:

```
typedef int T;

class TArray {
 protected:
    int _sz;
    T * _contents;

 public:
    TArray(int sz, int zeroed = 1)
        {
            _contents = sz ? new T[sz] : 0;
            _sz = sz;
            if (zeroed) memset(_contents, 0, sizeof(T)*sz);
        }
    ~TArray()
        { delete _contents; }

    T& operator[](int i)
        { return _contents[i]; }

    operator T *()
        { return _contents; }

    int size()
        { return sizeof(T) * _sz; }
} ;
```

The constructor builds an array of `sz` elements and optionally arranges for this array to be zeroed:

```
TArray ta(10);          // to get 10 zeroed elements
TArray ta(10, 0);       // to get 10 nonzeroed elements
```

The destructor gets rid of the array as you would expect.

`Operator  T*()` permits you to pass the array name as though it were simply a pointer to the elements.  This means that you can write:

```
T *tptr = ta;
if (ta) doSomething();
else if (!ta) doSomethingElse();
memset(ta, 0, ta.size());
```

The `operator[]` function returns a `T&` rather than a `T`. Returning a reference prevents a temporary object from being constructed, which means that you can write:

```
ta[5] = <new value>;
```

and the value ends up in the original `TArray` instance. C does not permit assigning to the result of a function call. In C++, function calls that return references may appear on the left-hand side of an assignment. `Operator[]` is an example of such a function.

### *Differences Between TArray and Real Arrays*

The major problem with this class is that there is no way to do array-style initialization. The definition

```
TArray ta = { 1, 2, 3, 4, 5 };
```

isn't legal C++ code. As a workaround to this problem, a constructor can be added that takes an array and a size that would permit you to write:

```
Static T _hiddenArray = { 1, 2, 3, 4, 5 };
TArray ta(_hiddenArray, sizeof(hiddenArray)/sizeof(T));
```

To do this, several changes need to be made. A new constructor is obviously needed, but in addition it is now necessary to remember whether the array was passed in or allocated in the heap so that the class knows whether or not to free it. The new class definition is:

```
class TArray {
 protected:
    int _sz;
    int _needsFree;
    T *_contents;
 public:
    TArray(int sz, int zeroed = 1)
        {
            _contents = sz ? new T[sz] : 0;
            _needsFree = 1;
            _sz = sz;
            if (zeroed) memset(_contents, 0, sizeof(T)*sz);
        }
    TArray(T *staticArray, int numElements)
        {
            _needsFree = 0;
            _contents = staticArray;
            _sz = numElements;
        }
    ~TArray()
        { if (_needsFree)
            delete _contents; }
    // ...
} ;
```

Another major difference between `TArray` and a C++ array of `T` is its behavior with respect to `sizeof()` and initialization functions:

```
TArray ta(5);
T native_ta[5];

sizeof(ta)   12
sizeof(native_ta)   20

memset(ta, 0, sizeof(ta));              // NOT what you want!!!!
memset(ta, 0, ta.size());               // okay
memset(native_ta, 0, sizeof(native_ta)); // okay
```

On the whole, the `TArray` class gets pretty close to the real thing.

### Performance

A couple of points should be made about this array class. First, it has minimal size overhead. The array class takes up precisely the same amount of memory as the built-in arrays supported by the language, plus four extra words: one for the size field, one for the pointer field, one to remember about deallocation, and one that gets eaten up by the memory allocator on your machine.

In addition, its only run-time overhead is at construction. In theory, all of the member functions get inlined, and a good compiler will peephole optimize away all of the overhead code that results from having to dereference the _contents member. The only hidden cost is the construction-time allocation of the array contents. For arrays that are allocated as locals, this construction overhead is unavoidable even for the language's built-in array type. For arrays that are allocated as global variables, the construction cost is incurred only once.

Or at least, that's how it ought to be if you have a reasonably good C++ compiler. Not being one to leave well enough alone, I decided to write a test program and find out if inlining really worked as advertised. I built an array of 1000 integers and a TArray of 1000 integers, initialized each with decreasing values from 1000 to 1, and ran a bubble sort over both arrays. The interesting part of the code was:

```
start = clock();

for (i = 0; i < ENTRIES; i++)
    Numbers[i] = ENTRIES - i;

for (i = 0; i < (ENTRIES-1); i++) {
    for (j = i; j < (ENTRIES-1); j++) {
        if (Numbers[j] < Numbers[j+1]) {
            int tmp = Numbers[j+1];
            Numbers[j+1] = Numbers[j];
            Numbers[j] = tmp;
        }
    }
}

stop = clock();
```

I was surprised to learn that the TArray version took three times as long as the native array version! A little investigation led to the realization that my compiler was based on the AT&T C++ translator. This version of the translator failed to inline the right-hand side of the comparison and assignment operators. The resulting function call overhead accounts for the extra execution time.

The bottom line to the performance numbers is that there exists a bug in the compiler. There is no reason why the compiler should not have inlined the right hand side of the comparison and assignment operators. In doing so, it would have exposed opportunities for other code optimizations that were lost because of the inlining failure.

Don't let this sort of problem discourage you. The chances are good that the bug isn't affecting your program's critical path. If you discover by profiling that it is, you can tune the code later. In addition, the chances are good that the compiler will be improved before your program is ready to ship. There are several C++ projects underway, and a few of them will be released soon. *Write your programs to the language, not to the implementation.* When the inliner is fixed (hopefully soon), the TArray version will be just as fast as the native version.

## 9.2   A Bounded Array Class

Given the TArray class, adding a bounds-checking feature is a very simple matter:

```
#include <assert.h>

class TBoundedArray : public TArray {
 public:
    TBoundedArray(int sz, int zeroed = 1)
    : TArray(sz, zeroed)
        { }

    TBoundedArray(T *staticArray, int numElements)
    : TArray(staticArray, numElements)
        { }

    ~TBoundedArray()
        { }

    T& operator[](int i)
        {
            assert(i < _sz);
            return _contents[i];
        }
} ;
```

When a user of TBoundedArray gives an array index that is too large, the call to assert() fails, resulting in a diagnostic and (on UNIX systems) a core dump that can be debugged to find the offending line of code. All of the bounds checking logic is performed inline, just as it would be in Pascal. A good compiler eliminates most of the compile-time overhead of the checks. When the program has been debugged to your satisfaction, the feature can be entirely turned off by compiling it with the NDEBUG macro defined, which disables assertion checking.

This bounds checking feature is not the answer to all problems, of course, because you can still obtain a pointer to the _contents field by writing &SomeArray[0] and manipulate the pointer without the benefit of bounds checking. This proves to be a very hard problem to solve without breaking a lot of things, and saving the malicious user from themselves isn't the purpose of the class. *Design for the common case.*

### *Performance*

Once again, I wrote a test program. This time, I wanted to compare the sorting time of TArray to TBoundedArray. On 1000 elements, the bounded array version ran in 592 ticks, versus 427 ticks for the unchecked version; a performance loss of less than 50 percent. In tight loop such as bubble sort, this is about what you should expect: the bounds checking introduces as many operations as the comparison and swap operations do.

Here again, the lack of complete inlining hurt, since the bounds checks were performed redundantly in several cases. Better inlining would have helped to eliminate this.

## 9.3   Improving the Design of TArray

Suppose that instead of T being a typedef for int, it is a typedef for a class:

```
typedef myClass T;
```

This class T has a constructor, and it is almost certainly wrong to zero the contents of the the array after these constructors have been run, because doing so will demolish the setup done by the constructor for T. On the other hand, you do want to be able to zero the class contents if the contents are of a fundamental type.

The answer to this problem is to leave the zeroing of things to the user of TArray. This means that the TArray constructor should be rewritten as:

```
TArray(int sz)
    {
        _contents = sz ? new T[sz] : 0;
        _sz = sz;
    }
```

This change has an impact on TBoundedArray. You now need to rewrite the constructor of TBoundedArray, too:

```
TBoundedArray(int sz)
 : TArray(sz)
      { }
```

In this case, you were lucky. Most changes to a base class require that the designs of any derived classes be re-examined.

### Iterative Design Is Important

In the first design of the TArray class, I had a reInit() function. ReInit() simply clobbered whatever was currently in the TArray instance and built a new _contents area. I deleted it from the class after deciding that this wasn't a good idea, because it invited users of TArray to reuse the data structure rather than making their code clear. It really isn't any harder to destroy the old one and build a new one. Adding an assignment operator would do the trick equally well in most cases, and would make the code simpler to understand.

Fortunately, my development group was in the process of trying to build something using the TArray class, and pointed out a fairly fundamental design oversight to me. Suppose you have a structure such as:

```
struct someStruct {
    int a;
    in nElements;
    myClass *classInstances;
} ;
```

You don't know how big it will be when someStruct is constructed, but you know that once initialized the number of elements won't change. You would like to take advantage of the bounds checking capabilities that TArray provides.

A quick look at TArray should convince you that the mechanism has already been built. What is needed is a way to construct an empty TArray and decide how big it should be later. Adding a member function does part of the trick:

```
TArray::init(int newSize)
{
    assert(!(_sz || _contents));
    _sz = newSize;
    _contents = new T[_sz];
}
```

This allows us to create a TArray and fill in the size later by saying:

```
TArray myArray(0);
// ...
myArray.init(newSize);
```

This addition substantially improves the utility of the TArray class without in any way compromising its safety. It's simply a problem that never occurred to me in the original design. It seems obvious, but most class designers never bother to test their classes in the environments where they will get used. They solve a single problem and publish the implementation, leaving others to discover that they could reuse the class, if only it had some capability that the original designer left out. Class design done right is an iterative process. If at first you think you succeeded, try again anyway.

Having added the TArray::init() member, it makes some sense now to have a default constructor that initializes the class to have zero elements. Once again, this change propagates into the TBoundedArray class:

```
TArray::TArray()
{
    _contents = 0;
    _sz = 0;
}

TBoundedArray::TBoundedArray()
: TArray()
{
}
```

## Exercises

1.  In the constructor for `TArray`, the call to `memset()` uses `ta.size()` rather than `sizeof(ta)`. Why is this?

2.  While testing the `TArray` class, I tried the following example:

    ```
    {
        T ta(10);
        if(ta)
            cout << "The (T *) operator works" << endl;

        const TArray& ta2 = ta;
        if(!ta2)
            cout << "The ! operator works" << endl;
    }
    ```

    The compiler complained that it was forced to use a non-const conversion in the test of `ta2`. How should this problem be fixed?

3.  Now that you think you know the answer to exercise 2, go and type it in and find out why it's wrong. There are two questions to be asked as a consequence. (A) How should the language rules for conversion resolution be changed so that this simple example works correctly? (B) Until it is fixed, what is the best way to work around the problem?

4.  The run-time allocation cost for `TArray` could be eliminated by making the size part of the type, and wiring it directly into the class. What is the cost of doing this, and how can the problem be reduced or eliminated altogether?

5.  The assertion check in `TBoundedArray` is wrong. Why? What change should be made to fix it?

6.  The `TArray` class lacks an assignment operator and a copy constructor. Add them.

7.  Now that you have added the assignment operator to `TArray`, `TBoundedArray` is broken. In what regard is this true, and what can be done to fix it? Should `TBoundedArray` have a copy constructor at all?

## 10

*Instead of trying to write a system which is just like last year's, only better implemented, one invariably tries to write an entirely new and more sophisticated system. Therefore you are in fact continually embarking on research.*

*— R. Barton*

# Dynamic Arrays

Occasionally you know that you need to build an array, but you don't know how big it will be. Managing the reallocation of such an array is an arduous and error-prone task. You would do well to embed it in a class that would take care of the details for you. Fortunately, building a dynamic array class is, on the face of it, not much more complicated than building the TBoundedArray class:

```
#include <assert.h>

class TDynamicArray : public TArray {
 protected:
    void grow(int newSize);
 public:
    TDynamicArray()
    : TArray()
        {  }

    TDynamicArray(int sz)
    : TArray(sz)
        {  }

    ~TDynamicArray();

    T& operator[](int i)
        {
            if(i >= sz)
                grow(i);
            return _contents[i];
        }
} ;
```

The interesting part of this implementation is the `grow()` function that actually performs the resizing:

```
void
TDynamicArray::grow(int newSize)
{
    int szNow = _sz;
    int contentsNow = _contents;

    _contents = new T[_sz = newSize];
    zero();

    while (szNow--)
        _contents[szNow] = contentsNow[szNow];

    delete contentsNow;
}
```

`TDynamicArray::grow()` preserves the old contents and extends the array to be big enough to hold the largest index that is referenced. You will see in a moment that in general, the method used to copy the array is not the right thing to do. There is a more immediate problem: `TDynamicArray` violates the principle of least amazement. It doesn't conform to the user's expectations.

In the `Tarray` class, the `_contents` field was guaranteed not to change once it was initialized. Because of this, it was acceptable to give out the value of `_contents` as a pointer to the base of the array. In `TDynamicArray`, resizing may cause the value of the `_contents` field to change. Any code that has kept a copy of the `_contents` pointer will end up with a pointer to random junk if the array is resized. There isn't much to be done about this problem, because you need to be able to give out the pointer so that `TDynamicArray` instances can be passed to routines that expect arrays. It is important, however, that this case is recognized and documented so that users of `TDynamicArray` do not receive rude surprises.

The right answer is necessarily specific to the environment in which the class is being used. Depending on how much rope you wish to offer your users, this problem might be sufficient reason to avoid exporting a way to get at the contents. A middle ground would be to export only an `operator int()`, which would permit boolean tests but not permit retention of a pointer value. Exporting `operator void *()` as well would be enough to permit routines such as `qsort()` to continue to work. Exporting the pointer as a `void *` helps to discourage users from trying to hang on to it for later use, since explicit conversion nis needed. Finally, you might decide to implement a `ptr()` member, in the hope that the need to invoke an unusual syntax would convey the need for caution to your users.

It is my opinion that the right answer in most cases lies in the combination of exporting `operator int()` and `operator void *()`. As a class designer, your objective is to make it easy to do the right things, and make it difficult to do things that are dangerous. If the user writes:

```
T *myTPointer = (T *) ((void *) ta);
```

they will probably wonder why the appropriate cast member function wasn't there in the first place. In examining the source of the class implementation, they will learn that the value is volatile. Undoubtedly, there will be occasions when the user needs to be able to get at the contents anyway. It seems a bad policy to prevent such access altogether.

## 10.1 The Problem with `TDynamicArray::grow()`

The original formulation of the `TArray` class was careful to define things in terms of `T`, which was a typedef. Suppose that instead of `T` being a typedef for `int`, you make it a typedef for a class:

```
typedef iostream T;
```

Take a closer look at what happens inside `TDynamicArray::grow()`.

```
int szNow = _sz;
```

No problem here.

```
int contentsNow = _contents;
```

Save the old array to make sure that it doesn't get lost in the shuffle. No problem here.

```
_contents = new T[_sz = newSize];
```

Construct some potentially large number of `iostream` instances, some of which will be overwritten when the old elements are copied back into the array.

```
zero();
```

Zero out the contents of the newly created array. Note that this might destroy the effects of the constructions that were just done if they initialize the elements to something other than zero.

```
while (szNow--)
    _contents[szNow] = contentsNow[szNow];
```

Copy some potentially large number of `iostream` instances, undoing the construction you just did for these elements.

```
delete contentsNow;
```

Delete all of the old versions.

Conceptually, the user only created the new objects, not the old ones. Running all of the constructors and destructors can be arbitrarily expensive, which is a good reason to avoid doing it. In addition, the constructors and destructors might attempt to do reference counting of other objects. You don't want to invoke all of the reference counting logic when you know you won't be changing any of the references.

What is needed is a way to allocate the new space, copy the old elements into it without invoking the assignment operator, run the default initializers only on the new elements, and free up the space the old elements used in such a way that the destructors will not be run on them. C++ provides a way to do this:

```
#define GROWRATE 1024

void
TDynamicArray::grow(int ndx)
{
    register void *oldContents = _contents;
    register int oldSz = _sz;
    register T *newBuf;
```

```
      while (_sz <= ndx)
        _sz += GROWRATE;

      register int nbytes = _sz * sizeof(T);
      newBuf = (T *) new char[nbytes];

      if(oldContents)
        memcpy(newBuf, oldContents, oldSz * sizeof(T));

      delete oldContents;

      /* now arrange for the new ones to get initialized:   */

      new(newBuf + oldSz) T[_sz - oldSz];
      _contents = (T *) newBuf;
   }
```

Because the new buffer is allocated as a vector of characters, no constructors are run; there is no default constructor for arrays of characters. Since the copy is done with `memcpy()`, no assignment operators are invoked to do the copy. `OldContents` is declared as `void *`, so the deallocation of the old buffer does not cause any destructors to be run. Finally, using the two-argument variety of the `new()` operator ensures that the default constructors get called for the new elements.

By the same logic that applied to building `grow()`, the `zero()` member function should almost certainly be renamed `reinit()`, and should be implemented by deleting the old buffer and allocating a new one to ensure that the proper destructors and constructors are run.

## 10.2  Generic Arrays

The `TArray` class and its descendants have some important limitations, but the classes seem to work well in practice. The only bad part is that a new class must be written for each new base object. While this is necessary to satisfy the constraints of the type system, it is a considerable amount of work to do each time you wish to build an array class. It should be clear how to do this after the number of examples you have already seen:

```
#define Array(type)   name2(Array,type)

#define MakeArray(ETYPE)                                   \
class Array(TYPE) {                                        \
 protected:                                               \
     int _sz;                                             \
     TYPE *_contents;                                     \
                                                          \
 public:                                                  \
    Array(type)(int sz)                                   \
        {                                                 \
             _contents = new TYPE[sz];                    \
             _sz = sz;                                    \
        }                                                 \
    ~Array(type)()                                        \
        { delete _contents; }                             \
                                                          \
    init()                                                \
        {                                                 \
             assert(!(_sz || _contents));                 \
             _sz = newSize;                               \
             _contents = new TYPE[_sz];                   \
        }                                                 \
                                                          \
    TYPE& operator[](int i)                               \
        { return _contents[i]; }                          \
                                                          \
    operator TYPE *()                                     \
        { return _contents; }                             \
                                                          \
    TYPE *operator&()                                     \
        { return _contents; }                             \
                                                          \
    int size()                                            \
        { return sizeof(TYPE) * _sz; }                    \
} ;
```

Given this macro, you can define an array class by writing:

```
MakeArray(int);
```

and create an instance of it by writing:

```
Array(int) myArray;
```

There is an unfortunate catch in using this style of class definition. The base type must be an identifier. To understand this, look at what happens if you write:

```
Array(char *)
```

The preprocessor comes along and happily turns this into a single line that looks like:

```
class char *Array { // ...
```

which is a syntax error. The solution to this problem is to get into the habit of making definitions for these types with a `typedef`:

```
typedef char *CharPtr;
Array(CharPtr);
```

works correctly.

## *Debugging Generic Classes*

Using macros to build generic classes has an unfortunate side effect. By the time the C++ compiler sees it, the entire class definition is on a single line. While this doesn't cause any trouble for the compiler, it stops C++ from giving helpful error messages. Suddenly, "Syntax error at line 42" could be a problem anywhere in the class.

Usually, it takes several attempts to get a class definition right. When you build a new generic class, you can work around the preprocessor problem by writing the class without the macro and testing it by hand:

```
#define Array(type)   name2(Array,type)

#define TYPE int

class Array(TYPE) {
 protected:
    int _sz;
    TYPE *_contents;
```

```
public:
    Array(type)(int sz)
        {
                _contents = new TYPE[sz];
                _sz = sz;
        }
    // ...
} ;
```

The only difference between this version and the macroized version is that this one is not part of a macro. When you have debugged the class to your satisfaction, add the macro definition and the backslash characters to macroize it. To help me with this procedure, I wrote a function for the GNU EMACS editor that would automatically insert and remove the backslashes.

Macroized classes will be used throughout the rest of this book.

## 10.3   Making BoundedArray Generic

Using a macro to generate the class name has a useful side effect: a derived class doesn't need to know exactly what scheme was used to build the base class name. To illustrate why generating the class name automatically is important, consider the problem of creating a generic BoundedArray class. In the original TBoundedArray, the class depended on being able to derive from TArray. While you could duplicate the code and eliminate the inheritance, it is very useful to be able to turn a BoundedArray into an Array when you hand it to a library routine that has already been tested on the Array classes.

The desire to inherit from the Array class means that the BoundedArray macro must know the name of the appropriate Array variant, which is why the name generation needs to be automatic. Here is the macro that defines BoundedArray:

```
#define BoundedArray(TYPE) name2(BoundedArray,TYPE)

#define MakeBoundedArray(TYPE)                                    \
class BoundedArray(TYPE)                                          \
    : public Array(TYPE){                                         \
 public:                                                          \
   BoundedArray(TYPE)(int sz)                                     \
    : Array(TYPE)(sz)                                             \
        { }                                                       \
                                                                 \
   ~BoundedArray(TYPE)();                                         \
                                                                 \
   TYPE& operator[](int i)                                        \
       {                                                          \
            assert(i < _sz);                                      \
            return _contents[i];                                  \
       }                                                          \
} ;
```

This class refers to the base class only using the declaration macro. If at some later point there is a name collision, the name of the `Array` class can be changed without impacting anything else in the code.

## Exercises

1.  Build a macroized version of the `TDynamicArray` class.

2.  The need to coerce the type system in order to grow an array is distasteful.  C avoids the need for this with the `realloc()` library routine.  Suggest a new operator that might be added to C++ to make growing objects in the heap easier.  What are the rules for construction and destruction of objects as a heap buffer is resized?

3.  A problem with dynamic arrays is that they aren't adequately bounds checked.  Ideally, a dynamic array would grow only when the new element is actually assigned a value.  Simply referencing the element shouldn't cause the array to grow.  This semantics can be achieved by introducing another object type.  Implement and test this variation on dynamic arrays.

4.  A useful variation on dynamic arrays is the sparse array.  Elements of a sparse array have a default value, and any element that has not been explicitly assigned contains this default value.  Typically, most values will have the default, so you want to store only the exceptions. Implement a sparse array class.

5.  There are several operations that work on fixed size arrays that don't work fully on variable size arrays because the array size can be changed.  An example of this is that indexing through the array by using a pointer and operator++ works only if the array size remains unchanged.  What other operations may not work if the array size changes?

*To iterate is human; to recurse divine.*
                                    *— Anonymous*

# 11

## Binary Trees

Like lists, binary trees are one of the basic data structures used frequently in everyday programming. Because they are so useful, this chapter is devoted to building a class for binary tree construction.

At its heart, a binary tree is a simple thing: it is an ordered collection of objects. In the usual case, no two nodes are permitted to have the same key value. When a position must be found for a new value, a search is done in the tree to find a slot for it by starting at the top and proceeding down the tree. Suppose the new item is $N$, and let $C$ be the current node in the tree. To find a place for $N$, the algorithm is simple:

>  1.   Let $C$ be the root of the tree.
>
>  2.   While $C$ is not an empty node:
>
>  >  2a.   If key($C$) < key($N$), set C to leftchild(C).
>  >  2b.   If key($C$) > key($N$), set C to rightchild(C).
>  >  2c.   If key($C$) == key($N$), signal an error.
>
>  3.   Insert $N$ at position $C$.

The net effect is that a new value threads it's way through the tree until a position for it is found:

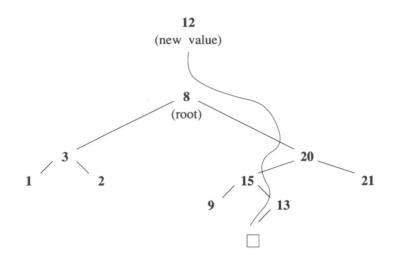

If the values are inserted in a random order, the tree will tend to stay balanced.

## 11.1   Implementing BinaryTree

The basic node structure of a binary tree is straightforward:

```
struct BinaryTreeNode {
    BinaryTreeNode *left, *right;
    int value;
public:
    BinaryTreeNode(int newValue)
        { left = right = 0;  value = newValue; }
    ~BinaryTreeNode()
        { }
} ;
```

The tree class itself is:

```
class BinaryTree {
    BinaryTreeNode *root;
public:
    BinaryTree()
        { root = 0; }
    ~BinaryTree();

    int insert(int value);
    int lookup(int value);
} ;
```

The `lookup()` function checks to see if a number is already in the tree, returning 1 if it is and zero otherwise:

```
int
BinaryTree::lookup(int value)
{
    BinaryTreeNode *cur = root;
    while (cur) {
        if (cur->value == value)
            return 1;
        else if (cur->value < value)
            cur = cur->left;
        else
            cur = cur->right;
    }

    return 0;
}
```

The `insert()` function is a little bit more complicated, because it has to look ahead to see if it is about to fall off of the bottom of the tree. Like the `lookup()` routine, `insert()` returns 1 on success and zero on failure.

```
int
BinaryTree::insert(int value)
{
    BinaryTreeNode *cur = root;
    if (cur == 0) {
        root = new BinaryTreeNode(value);
        return 1;
    }

    for(;;) {
        if (cur->value == value)
            return 0;
        else if (value < cur->value) {
            if (cur->left) {
                cur = cur->left;
                continue;
            }
            cur->left = new BinaryTreeNode(value);
            return 1;
        }
```

```
                   else {
                       if (cur->right) {
                           cur = cur->right;
                           continue;
                       }
                       cur->right = new BinaryTreeNode(value);
                       return 1;
                   }
               }
           }
```

The complexity in the insertion routine comes from the need to look ahead at each move and see if the next node down the tree exists.

### *A Little Indirection is a Good Thing*

While the `insert()` routine given above works, it can be simplified by introducing an extra level of indirection. Instead of keeping a pointer to the current node, suppose that `insert()` kept a pointer *to the pointer*, as in

```
BinaryTreeNode **nodePtr = &root;
```

If this indirection pointer is used, the code becomes more compact and consequently easier to understand:

```
int
BinaryTree::insert(int value)
{
    BinaryTreeNode **cur = &root;

    while (*cur) {
        if (value == (*cur)->value)
            return 0;
        else if (value < (*cur)->value)
            cur = &((*cur)->left);
        else
            cur = &((*cur)->right);
    }

    (*cur) = new BinaryTreeNode(value);
    return 1;
}
```

You could even think about having the lookup routine use the same code by separating the search code from the lookup and insertion code:

```
BinaryTreeNode **
BinaryTree::findNode(int value)
{
    BinaryTreeNode **cur = &root;

    while (*cur) {
        if (value == (*cur)->value)
            return cur;
        else if (value < (*cur)->value)
            cur = &((*cur)->left);
        else
            cur = &((*cur)->right);
    }

    return cur;
}

int
BinaryTreeNode::lookup(value)
{
    BinaryTreeNode **nodePtr = findNode(value);
    return (*nodePtr != 0);
}

int
BinaryTreeNode::insert(value)
{
    BinaryTreeNode **nodePtr = findNode(value);
    if (*nodePtr == 0) {
        *nodePtr = new BinaryTreeNode(value);
        return 1;
    }
    else
        return 0;
}
```

This particular compression of the code probably isn't a good idea. In addition to introducing function call overhead into both procedures, it slows down the lookup process by forcing it to pay the cost of looking ahead at each step in the search, which lookup() doesn't need to do. Keeping the two algorithms separate has the added advantage that you could derive a balanced binary tree class from BinaryTree and only have to override the insertion member. In addition, this derivation possibility suggests that the insertion and deletion members should be virtual:

```
class BinaryTree {
    BinaryTreeNode *root;
public:
    BinaryTree()
        { root = 0; }
    ~BinaryTree();

    virtual int insert(int value);
    virtual int remove(int value);
    int lookup(int value);
} ;
```

Implementing the `remove()` routine is left as an exercise for the end of the chapter.

### Deleting the Binary Tree

One operation still needs to be implemented: tree deletion. When a `BinaryTree` is deleted, it and all of its book-keeping nodes should be deallocated. The obvious algorithm is recursive, and is most easily done with a helper function:

```
void BinaryTree::deleteNode(BinaryTreeNode *node)
{
    if (node->left)
        deleteNode(node->left);
    if (node->right)
        deleteNode(node->right);
    delete node;
}

BinaryTree::~BinaryTree()
{
    deleteNode(root);
}
```

## 11.2   Making BinaryTree Generic

The `BinaryTree` class has the unfortunate property that it keeps copies of all of the values stored in it. If the objects are large, this can be expensive. In addition, the `BinaryTree` class only knows how to store integers, and there are obviously other things that you might like to put in a `BinaryTree`. A more generic form of the class is needed.

The first step in turning `BinaryTree` into a generic class is to have it keep pointers to objects rather than objects themselves:

```
struct BinaryTreeNode {
    BinaryTreeNode *left, *right;
    void *value;
public:
    BinaryTreeNode(void *newValue)
        { left = right = 0;  value = newValue; }
    ~BinaryTreeNode()
        { }
} ;
```

The problem with this is that the pointer to the value is a pointer to an object of unknown type. `BinaryTree` has no way to know how to compare two objects. A comparison function needs to be supplied:

```
typedef int (*ComparisonFunction)(void *, void *);

class BinaryTree {
    BinaryTreeNode *root;
    ComparisonFunction  _compare;
public:
    BinaryTree(ComparisonFunction compare)
        { root = 0; _compare = compare; }
    ~BinaryTree();

    virtual void *insert(void *value);
    virtual int remove(int value);
    void *lookup(void *value);
} ;
```

When the `lookup()` and `insert()` routines are called, the comparison function is passed the addresses of the objects to be compared. The comparison function should return a result less than, equal to, or greater than 0 as the first object is less than, equal to, or greater than the second. If, for example, you intended to store strings in a `BinaryTree`, the comparison function might be:

```
int CompareStrings(void *v1, void *v2)
{
    char *s1 = (char *) v1, *s2 = (char *) v2;
    return strcmp(s1, s2);
}
```

The `lookup()` function needs to be modified to use this comparison function:

```
void *
BinaryTree::lookup(void *value)
{
    BinaryTreeNode *cur = root;
    while (cur) {
        int result = (*_compare)(cur->value, value);
        if (!result)
            return cur->value;
        else if (result < 0)
            cur = cur->left;
        else
            cur = cur->right;
    }

    return 0;
}
```

The usual approach to handling comparisons is to have multiple comparison routines; one for less-than, another for greater-than, and a third for equal-to.  Using a single comparison routine to handle all of these cases eliminates many unnecessary calls to the comparison routines.  Eliminating these extra function calls can substantially improve the speed of the search routine.

The `lookup()` routine has also been modified to return a useful piece of information: the old value.  This permits a binary tree client towrite:

```
struct Key {
    int someInterestingKey;
} ;
struct CompleteValue : public Key {
    CompleteValueContents moreStuff;
} ;
```

An object can be looked up and compared by key without having to generate the whole value.

The rewritten insertion function is:

```
void *
BinaryTree::insert(void *value)
{
    BinaryTreeNode **cur = &root;

    while (*cur) {
        int result = (*_compare)(value, (*cur)->value);
        if (result == 0)
            return (*cur)->value;
        else if (result < 0)
            cur = &((*cur)->left);
        else
            cur = &((*cur)->right);
    }

    (*cur) = new BinaryTreeNode(value);
    return value;
}
```

As in `lookup()`, the comparison routine is called only once. Note that this version of `insert()` returns the object found. It is no longer a failure to insert something twice. The second time an object is inserted with the same key, the original object is returned. The new interface provides enough information for a client to retain the original insert-once logic, but imposes fewer constraints on the client.

## 11.3  Handling Expensive Comparisons

Sometimes you have an object type that has a comparison function, but the comparison function is expensive to run. C character strings are expensive to compare, because the `strcmp()` function is forced to compare characters until one or the other string ends or there is a difference between the strings. As the tree of strings gets deeper, the number of characters that need to be compared increases.

If you don't care about keeping the strings in sorted order, there is a way to improve the situation. Suppose that instead of storing the string in the `BinaryTree`, you store an object that has a signature for the string and a pointer to the actual string:

```
struct StringPlaceHolder {
    int signature;
    char *string;
} ;
```

The signature is an integer value computed from the string. The idea is to come up with a value that is easy to compare but cheap to compute. Strings are usually words, and in most languages there are common prefixes and suffixes. A good signature function will compute from both the start and the end of the string to make sure that this doesn't cause signatures to "cluster." A good signature function for English words is:

```
int StringSignature(char * string)
{
    int i;
    int len = strlen(string);
    int signature = 0;

    for (i = 0; i < (len+1)/2; i++)
    {
        signature = signature * 27 + string[i];
        signature = signature * 27 + string[len - 1 - i];
    }
    return signature;
}
```

The comparison function for strings with signatures can be written as:

```
int CompareStringPlaceHolder(void *v1, void *v2)
{
    StringPlaceHolder *s1 = (char *) v1, *s2 = (char *) v2;

    if (s1->signature != s2->signature)
        return s1->signature - s2->signature;
    return strcmp(s1, s2);
}
```

Most of the comparisons won't need to call the more expensive `strcmp()` routine. The signature computation generates different results for words with the same prefix, so strings with the same signature will usually differ near the beginning of the strings. This means that when `strcmp()` is called it does less work to arrive at an answer. These changes combine to improve the search speed by a large factor.

## Exercises

1.  Implement a balanced binary tree class as described in Knuth's *The Art of Computer Programming*. Can this class be derived from the BinaryTree class?

2.  Write a remove() function for the BinaryTree class.

3.  Implement the remove() function for balanced binary trees.

3.  The important facts about the string signature function in this chapter are that it works from both sides of the string (this eliminates the effects of prefixes and suffixes) and that it multiplies by 27, which is relatively prime to both the number of letters in the lower case alphabet and the number of values possible in a byte. Suggest a better algorithm. Run your function and the one given against a sizeable dictionary of words to test how evenly it distributes its numbers.

4.  The string signature function does not preserve ordering of the strings. This means that the BinaryTree implementation performs fast lookups, but no longer keeps its elements in order, which defeats one of the key advantages of binary trees. Suggest a string signature function that keeps the strings in order.

5.  Calculate how much memory overhead there is for each item in the binary tree. Remember to include the overhead from the memory manager on your system. Are there other storage techniques which offer fast lookup but do not have so much overhead?

6.  A problem with the BinaryTree class is that the deletion algorithm is recursive. If your system doesn't have a lot of stack space (on a Macintosh®, for example), this can be a problem. It is possible to write a tree deletion algorithm that doesn't have this problem by using the left and right child pointers to do the backtracking. Implement such an algorithm.

*Every interesting program has at least one variable, one branch, and one loop.*
— *A. Perlis*

*And at least one bug!*

— *C. Strachey*

# 12

# Hash Tables

The project that I have been working on most recently is a client/server application. In the usual case, there is a single centralized server that provides services to a number of clients. Clients use a network protocol to ask the server to create or access objects on their behalf. These structures are called *resources*. Conceptually, all of the clients together form the application, so the resources created by one client are visible to the others. Because the clients and the server are distinct processes, resources must be named in a way that works across process boundaries. To keep the protocol simple, it is important that these resource names be fixed-size objects.

All of the objects live in the server, so you might use the addresses of the objects as their names. To create a resource, a message must be sent to the server to create the object, and a response returned to provide the address. However, this isn't a good choice from the standpoint of protocol design, because it requires a round trip between the client and the server. More importantly, a client could generate an incorrect address, and the server has no way to double-check the value before it is used. Worst of all, it is very likely that as objects are allocated and freed in the server the same address will come to name two objects. For the names to be useful, they must never be reused.

What you really want is to assign a unique 32 bit integer to each object, and remember what objects have been created and which clients are using each of them.  The challenge is to come up with a fast way to get from the name to the resource itself.  This is an ideal problem for hash tables.

## 12.1   Hash Table Basics

The concept of a hash table is straightforward.  Suppose you have a collection of strings, such as words in a spelling database.  Given some arbitrary string from an outside source, you would like a quick way to look it up in your collection.  In principle, of course, you could go through the whole collection and compare each of the items to the new one.  If you have thousands of strings this could take a while.

Ideally, you would like to find a cheap way to narrow the search before you start to do all of the comparisons.  This is what a hash table does.  The idea is to divide your items into $N$ groups, which are traditionally referred to as *buckets*.  Having decided what the value for $N$ is, you can then invent a function that takes an arbitrary item as input and generates a number between 1 and $N$.  This function is called a *hash function*.  The hash function can generate the same number for two different objects (indeed, hashing depends on the fact that it does so).  Two identical objects *must* generate the same value.

When you put an object into the collection, you compute this number and insert it into the appropriate bucket.  When you go to compare a new object against the existing objects, you run the hash function on the new object to find out which bucket to search.  If you have the right balance between the number of buckets and the number of items in each bucket, you can avoid doing a lot of comparisons, making the search very fast.

A good hash function distributes the items evenly among the buckets.  As a result, the choice of a function depends on the nature of the data items.  Picking a good function for computing hash values is an interesting problem, and considerable research has been devoted to it.  A full treatment of the mathematics of hash functions is beyond the scope of this book.  An excellent description of the nature of the problem and the guidelines for what makes a good hash function can be found in Knuth's *The Art of Computer Programming, Vol. 3: Sorting and Searching*.  The good news is that hash functions do not need to be perfect. In practice, sometimes sloppy ones work very well.

### What's in a Hash Table?

Each bucket in the table is implemented as a doubly linked list. In addition to the `next` and `prev` pointers, each item has a 32 bit id and a pointer to the object associated with that id.

```
struct HashEntry {
    unsigned long key;      /* hash key */
    void            *value;
    HashEntry       *next, *prev;

    HashEntry(unsigned long newkey)
        { key = newkey; next = 0; prev = 0; }
    ~HashEntry()
        {
            if (next) next->prev = prev;
            if (prev) prev->next = next;
        }
} ;


typedef HashEntry* HashEntryPtr;
```

The hash table itself has three interesting operations: `lookup()` checks the table to see if an item exists in it already, the `insert()` operation installs a new object into the table, and the `remove()` function correspondingly removes an object. Putting all of this together, the basic class is:

```
const NBUCKETS = 4096;

class HashTable {
    HashEntryPtr bucket[NBUCKTS];

    int hash(unsigned long key)
public:
    HashTable();
    ~HashTable();

    void add(unsigned long key, void *object);
    void *lookup(unsigned long key);
    void remove(unsigned long key);
    void mapcar(void (*f)(HashEntryPtr));
} ;
```

## How Many Buckets?

How many buckets the table should have is very dependent on the number of objects you expect to have to deal with. The more buckets there are, the fewer comparisons will be needed to locate the object of interest. On the other hand, each bucket takes up space. A reasonable rule of thumb is four objects to a bucket, so this definition can handle16,384 ($2^{13}$) objects.

The decision is a practical one. At this size, the bucket pointers eat up 16K of memory on most machines, and the 16K objects require 32 bytes of memory apiece, or half a megabyte of data just to keep them in the hash table. If you have more objects than this, it may be appropriate to consider other data structures.

Putting all of this together, we can write the constructor and destructor for the HashTable class.

```
HashTable::HashTable()
{
    for(int i = 0; i < NBUCKETS; i++)
        bucket[i] = 0;
}

HashTable::~HashTable()
{
    for(int i = 0; i < NBUCKETS; i++) {
        HashEntryPtr p = bucket[i];

        while(p) {
            bucket[i] = p->next;
            delete p;
            p = bucket[i];
        }
    }
}
```

## Choosing a Hash Function

Hash functions are difficult things to choose. A good one distributes the objects evenly over the buckets, which means that the hash function is sensitive to the number of buckets we have. If the names are generated sequentially, it might be enough to simply divide the 32-bit name by 4 and mask off the extra bits.  If a better distribution is required, the following hash function might be better:

```
int
HashTable::hash(register unsigned long key)
{
    unsigned const RESOURCE_ID_MASK = 0xfffff;

    key &= RESOURCE_ID_MASK;

    return ((int)(0x7FF & (key ^ (key>>11)))));
}
```

This function is adapted from the one found in the X server.  As a challenge, see if you can come up with a better one.

## 12.2  Implementing the Interface

The public interface of the `HashTable` class needs to be implemented. The most straightforward one to implement is `HashTable::lookup()`:

```
void *
HashTable::lookup(register unsigned long key)
{
    int whichBucket = hash(key);

    register HashEntryPtr p = bucket[whichBucket];

    while(p) {
        if (p->key == key)
            break;
        p = p->next;
    }

    if (!p)
        return 0;

    return p->value;
}
```

Adding new elements isn't all that much more complicated, but should be broken up into two functions:

```
HashEntryPtr
HashTable::addElement(register unsigned long key, void *value)
{
    register int whichBucket = hash(key);

    register HashEntryPtr p = new HashEntry(key);

    p->next = bucket[whichBucket];
    if (bucket[whichBucket])
        bucket[whichBucket]->prev = p;
    bucket[whichBucket] = p;

    return p;
}

void
HashTable::add(register unsigned long key, void *value)
{
    HashEntryPtr p = addElement(key);
    p->value = value;
}
```

It should be an error to add the same element more than once to a single
`HashTable`. This means that before adding a new element, you need to
check if the old one exists. The lookup is now being done in two places,
which strongly suggests rewriting the lookup as a separate procedure:

```
HashEntryPtr
HashTable::searchBucketFor(register HashEntryPtr p,
                           register unsigned long key)
{
    while(p) {
        if (p->key == key)
            break;
        p = p->next;
    }
    return p;
}
```

Both `HashTable::lookup()` and `HashTable::add()` can be rewritten to
use the new procedure:

```
void *
HashTable::lookup(register unsigned long key)
{
    int whichBucket = hash(key);

    HashEntryPtr p =
        searchBucketFor(bucket[whichBucket], key);

    if (!p)
        return 0;

    return p->value;
}

void
HashTable::add(register unsigned long key, void *value)
{
    int whichBucket = hash(key);

    HashEntryPtr p =
        searchBucketFor(bucket[whichBucket], key);
    assert(!p)

    p = addElement(key);
    p->value = value;
}
```

Finally, you need to be able to remove an existing element. Here again the separation of the search routine proves useful:

```
void
HashTable::remove(unsigned long key)
{
    int whichBucket = hash(key);

    HashEntryPtr p =
        searchBucketFor(bucket[whichBucket], key);
    if(!p)
        return;

    if(bucket[whichBucket] == p)
        bucket[whichBucket] = p->next;

    delete p;
}
```

The completed class definition is:

```
const NBUCKETS = 4096;

class HashTable {
    HashEntryPtr bucket[NBUCKETS];

    HashEntryPtr addElement(unsigned long key);
    HashEntryPtr searchBucketFor(HashEntryPtr p,
                                    unsigned long key);
    hash(unsigned long);
public:
    HashTable();
    ~HashTable();
    void add(unsigned long key, void *value);
    void *lookup(unsigned long key);
    void remove(unsigned long key);
} ;
```

## 12.3   Extending the Interface

Having described the basic version of the HashTable class, a few
functional improvements come to mind.  Occasionally, you will want to
use a HashTable not just as a fast mechanism for looking things up, but as
a collection of objects.  As an example, consider having a HashTable for
each client.  When a client has a reference to a resource, the resource id
and a pointer to the resource appear in the HashTable.

Clients don't always exit gracefully, and when they do exit, you would
like to be sure that all of their resources are freed appropriately.  What you
want to do at this point is to iterate over all of the members of the
HashTable and free them.

Adding such a member function is straightforward.  The idea is that you
pass it a pointer to the function you want to have it call on each element of
the HashTable:

```
typedef void (*MapFun)(void *);

void
HashTable::map(MapFun f)
{
    for(int i = 0; i < NBUCKETS; i++) {
        HashEntryPtr p = bucket[i];

        while(p) {
            f(p->value);
            p = p->next;
        }
    }
}
```

Notice that the `HashTable::map()` routine knows nothing at all about the types of the objects that have been hashed, which helps make the routine more generally useful. The cost of this is a loss of type checking, a problem we shall come back to in a moment.

As an example of how this might be used, consider the debugging problem of wanting to print a list of all of the items in a `HashTable`:

```
extern HashTable ItemTable;

static void
PrintItem(ItemType *)
{
    // ... code to print up the item ...
}

void
DebuggingPrintItems()
{
    ItemTable.map((MapFun) PrintItem);
}
```

The case of the dying client can be handled similarly:

```
extern HashTable ResourceTable;

static void
FreeResource(Resource *)
{
    if (--r->refcount == 0)
        delete r;
}
```

```
void
FreeClientResources()
{
    ResourceTable.map((MapFun) FreeResource);
}
```

## 12.4   Generic Hash Tables

The basic version of the `HashTable` class assumes that the hash key is an unsigned long.  In a more general hashing scheme this is an unacceptable constraint.  Consider, for example, the problem of hashing strings.

The generic version of the `HashTable` class is somewhat more complicated than any of the generic classes in previous chapters, primarily because its implementation is so large.  The class has a large number of component types, so to reduce the number of errors in building the macro, it is helpful to define some supporting macros:

```
#include <generic.h>

#ifndef NBUCKETS
#define NBUCKETS 4096
#endif

#define HashTable(KEYTYPE)    name2(HashTable_,KEYTYPE)
#define HashEntry(KEYTYPE)    name2(HashEntry_,KEYTYPE)
#define HashEntryPtr(KEYTYPE) name2(HashEntryPtr_,KEYTYPE)
```

The hash table construction macro needs to construct not only the hash table class, but the structure for the table entries as well:

```
#define MakeHashTable(KEYTYPE)                                  \
struct HashEntry(KEYTYPE) {                                     \
    KEYTYPE                 key;  /* hash key */                \
    void                    *value;                             \
    HashEntry(KEYTYPE) *next, *prev;                            \
                                                               \
    HashEntry(KEYTYPE) (KEYTYPE newkey)                         \
        { key = newkey; next = 0; prev = 0; }                  \
    ~HashEntry(KEYTYPE) ()                                      \
        {                                                      \
            if (next) next->prev = prev;                       \
            if (prev) prev->next = next;                       \
        }                                                      \
} ;                                                             \
```

```
typedef HashEntry(KEYTYPE)* HashEntryPtr(KEYTYPE);             \
                                                              \
class HashTable(KEYTYPE) {                                     \
    HashEntryPtr(KEYTYPE) bucket[NBUCKETS];                    \
                                                              \
    int (*_compare)(KEYTYPE, KEYTYPE);                        \
    HashEntryPtr(KEYTYPE) addElement(KEYTYPE key);            \
    HashEntryPtr(KEYTYPE)                                      \
        searchBucketFor(HashEntryPtr(KEYTYPE) p,             \
                        KEYTYPE key);                         \
    int hash(KEYTYPE);                                        \
                                                              \
public:                                                       \
    HashTable(KEYTYPE)(int (*)(KEYTYPE, KEYTYPE));            \
    ~HashTable(KEYTYPE)();                                    \
    void add(KEYTYPE key, void * value);                     \
    void *lookup(KEYTYPE key);                               \
    void remove(KEYTYPE key);                                \
    void mapcar(void (*f)(HashEntryPtr(KEYTYPE)));           \
} ;
```

With one exception, the implementation follows the same basic pattern as in previous generic classes:

```
#define ImplementHashTable(KEYTYPE)                           \
HashTable(KEYTYPE)::HashTable(KEYTYPE)                        \
            (int (*compare)(KEYTYPE, KEYTYPE))               \
{                                                             \
    _compare = compare;                                      \
    for(int i = 0; i < NBUCKETS; i++)                        \
        bucket[i] = 0;                                        \
}                                                             \
// ... rest of HashTable Members...
```

The exception is the hash routine, which is most easily supplied by the user, and therefore is not included in the macroized version of the class.

A complete listing of the generic `HashTable` class is given at the end of the book.

### *Building a HashTable*

Given these two macros, you can now define a `HashTable` over any type. A complete implementation requires a header file and a source file that use the `MakeHashTable` and `ImplementHashTable` macros, respectively. Two implementation-specific functions are also needed: the hash function and the function to compare two keys. These are defined by the user. To show how it all fits together, you can use the macros to build a `HashTable` of unsigned longs, which is essentially the original `HashTable` implementation.

```
// ... in the header file ...
typedef unsigned long u_long;
MakeHashTable(u_long);

// ... in the implementation file ...
ImplementHashTable(u_long);

int
HashTable(u_long)::hash(register u_long key)
{
    unsigned const RESOURCE_ID_MASK = 0xfffff;

    key &= RESOURCE_ID_MASK;

    return ((int)(0x7FF & (key ^ (key>>11))));
}
```

Having done the implementation and class definition, a `HashTable` can be declared by writing:

```
int
ul_compare(unsigned long ul1, unsigned long ul2)
{
    return ul1 == ul2;
}
HashTable(u_long) myTable(ul_compare);
```

The argument to the `HashTable` constructor is a pointer to a function that compares two keys.

## Exercises

1. In the generic `HashTable` class, the user-supplied hash function is a member of the class while the similarly supplied comparison function is not. What prompted this decision? Was it a good one?

2. One problem with the design for `HashTable` in this chapter is that it is very expensive when there are only a few objects to be hashed. It would be relatively easy to redesign the `HashTable` to grow as more objects are added. Design and implement a version of `HashTable` to do this.

3. When the hash table changes size, it is typically wise to switch hash functions. Suggest a hash function that addresses this issue.

4. One way to improve the performance of a hash table lookup is to implement the buckets as small binary trees, reducing the number of comparisons that need to be done in walking the bucket contents. The obvious alternative is to design a hash table that adaptively resizes itself as the need arises. What are the trade-off issues in choosing between these options, and where is the break-even point (i.e., how many items need to be in a bucket on average for it to matter if the bucket is a binary tree)?

5. Calculate how much memory overhead there is for each item in the hash table. Remember to include the overhead from the memory manager on your system. How does this compare to the per-item overhead of binary trees?

*Bloody instructions which being learned,*
*return to plague the inventor.*
                    *— W. Shakespeare, MacBeth*

# 13

# A Pointer Class

Memory management has simultaneously been one of the banes and features of C. On one hand, the simplicity of `malloc()` and `free()` has a certain appeal. On the other hand, the simplicity of the model has a cost: it is very easy to make memory errors and very hard to fix them once they have been made.

C++ inherits all of the problems and benefits of the C memory management model. The names have changed, but the innocent are hardly protected. Fortunately, C++ provides most of the tools you need to do something about this. This chapter introduces a class that mimics pointers, and provides an in-depth exploration of C++ operator overloading.

## 13.1  The Basic Version

Creating a safe pointer class is a fair bit of work. The first step is to create a class that looks and feels to the programmer just like a C++ pointer, and then think about how to enhance it. If you have a pointer to type *T*, the services that the pointer provides are:

- assignment from other objects of type `T *`,

- dereferencing to get to an object of type `T`,

- `operator->`, a shorthand for dereferencing,

- `operator[]`, which provides array indexing,

- cast to type `void *`,

- addition, to increment through an array,

- subtraction, to decrement back through an array,

- pre and post increment and decrement (operators ++ and --),

- conversion to integer and unary ! for use in conditional expressions.

A class can get pretty close to doing all of this, and can help eliminate dangling pointer problems.

To begin with, simply build a class that handles one type correctly. On the face of it, this shouldn't be too difficult a task:

```
class T;

class Pointer_T {
    T * _ptr;

  public:
    Pointer_T()
      { _ptr = 0; }
    Pointer_T(T *t)
      { _ptr = t; }
    Pointer_T(Pointer_T& pt)
      { _ptr = pt._ptr; }

    T *ptr()
      { return _ptr; }
    operator T *()
      { return _ptr; }

    operator int()
      { return (int) _ptr; }
    int operator !()
      { return !_ptr; }

    Pointer_T& operator=(Pointer_T& pt)
      { _ptr = pt._ptr; }
    Pointer_T& operator=(T *t);
      { _ptr = t; }
```

```
    T& operator[](int i)
        { return _ptr[i]; }
    T *operator->()
        { return _ptr; };
    T& operator*()
        { return *_ptr; };
} ;
```

In principle, this seems like it should do the job. Unfortunately, it doesn't compile. The reason is that `operator[]` needs to know the size of `T`, which isn't defined. Until the definition of `T` has been provided, the pointer class as shown won't work. This is unfortunate because it is perfectly legal to write

```
    T *myptr;
```

when `T` has not been defined. In my view, this is a bug in the C++ language. It shouldn't matter that the size is not known at the declaration of the pointer class. What is important is that everything needed is known when the function is used. However, this isn't the way the language works, and it falls to us as programmers to find a way to work around this particular problem.

The solution is not as bad as it may seem. The following class definition *will* compile quite happily:

```
    class T;

    class Pointer_T {
        T *_ptr;
     public:
        Pointer_T()
            { _ptr = 0; }
        Pointer_T(T *t)
            { _ptr = t; }

        Pointer_T(Pointer_T& pt)
            { _ptr = pt._ptr; }

        T *ptr()
            { return _ptr; }
        operator T *()
            { return _ptr; }
```

```
operator int()
  { return (int) _ptr; }
int operator !()
  { return !_ptr; }

Pointer_T& operator=(Pointer_T& pt)
  { _ptr = pt._ptr; }
Pointer_T& operator=(T *t);
  { _ptr = t; }

T *operator->()
  { return _ptr; };
T& operator*()
  { return *_ptr; };
T& operator[](int i);       // out of line to keep
                            // the compiler happy.  YUCK!
} ;
```

The question now is: Is there a way to implement the `operator[]`
function so that it is still inlined?  The answer is yes.  Once the definition
of T has been seen, you can write:

```
inline Pointer_T&
Pointer_T::operator[](int i)
{ return _ptr[i]; }
```

Some other operators have not been defined that work on pointers.  Real C
pointers can take part in arithmetic operations, such as addition and
subtraction.  Leaving these out was a deliberate choice.  With the addition
and subtraction operators removed, it is possible to use the pointer class
for garbage collection.  The `operator[]` function should probably be
removed as well.  Since the pointer class can be converted to a true pointer
on demand, this isn't an unreasonable problem in practice.  Eliminating
the `operator[]`  member also makes it possible to compile the class
without defining the base type.

## 13.2   The Problem with Operator++

In spite of the fact that I have elected to exclude the arithmetic operators,
there is a special problem with `operator++` and `operator--` that deserves
note.  If you take a look at the C++ version 2.0 language reference manual,
you will see that the behavior of these operators is the same regardless of

whether the user said "++x" or "x++". The operator is applied as a preincrement or predecrement operator.

The code fragment

```
{
  Pointer_T t1, t2;
  *t1++ = *t2++
}
```

copies the wrong object!

Regrettably, there is no workaround for this problem in C++ version 2.0.[4] There is a way to protect yourself from it, however. *Always make the return type of* `operator++` *and* `operator--` *be* `void`. This will ensure that the user of your pointer class will get a syntax error when they write this example, and force them to write a version that C++ will handle correctly. It also means that when this problem is fixed (Bjarne is thinking about it even as I write), no existing code will be broken by the change. This is another application of the principle of least amazement.

If the return type of `operator++` is void, the example above will cause a syntax error, which is the best you can hope for in this situation. As a general matter, it is better to somehow make potentially wrong usage into a compile-time error than to implement it thinking that people will understand and not get caught. In real life, users almost never understand these subtleties, and they invariably get caught. Better to force the code to be written explicitly:

---

[4]  The problem has been resolved in C++ version 2.1, by introducing two new operators for postincrement and postdecremement. `operator++(int)` implements the postincrement operation and `operator--(int)` defines postdecrement. Versions of C++ that implement these operators should be available soon that handle these operators.

```
{
  Pointer_T t1, t2;
  *t1 = *t2
  t1++; t2++;
}
```

## 13.3   Allocating and Deallocating

Allocating objects for the new pointer class looks just like it always did:

```
{
  Pointer_T t1;
  t1 = new T;
}
```

Deallocating, on the other hand, doesn't do what you expect at all:

```
{
  Pointer_T t1;
  t1 = new T;
  // ...
  delete t1;
}
```

Surprise!  This is a syntax error.  The `delete` operator wants to be handed
a pointer.  Fortunately, you can create a `delete` operator that works
correctly by global overloading:

```
void
delete(Pointer_T&)
{
    delete pt._ptr;
}
```

This function needs to be a friend function of the `Pointer_T` class.  Now
the example works as expected.

## 13.4   Generic Pointers

The pointer class can easily be made generic by re-packaging it as a
macro:

```
#include <generic.h>
#define Ptr(T)   name2(Pointer_,T)

#define MakePtr(T)                                    \
     friend delete(Ptr(T)&)                           \
class Ptr(T) {                                        \
     T *_ptr;                                         \
                                                      \
 public:                                              \
     Ptr(T)()                                         \
        { _ptr = 0; }                                 \
     Ptr(T)(T *t)                                     \
        { _ptr = t; }                                 \
     Ptr(T)(Ptr(T)& pt)                               \
        { _ptr = pt._ptr; }                           \
                                                      \
     T *ptr()                                         \
        { return _ptr; }                              \
     operator T *()                                   \
        { return _ptr; }                              \
                                                      \
     operator int()                                   \
        { return (int) _ptr; }                        \
     int operator !()                                 \
        { return !_ptr; }                             \
                                                      \
     Ptr(T)& operator=(Ptr(T)& pt)                    \
        { _ptr = pt._ptr; }                           \
     Ptr(T)& operator=(T *t);                         \
        { _ptr = t; }                                 \
                                                      \
     T *operator->()                                  \
        { return _ptr; };                             \
     T& operator*()                                   \
        { return *_ptr; };                            \
} ;
```

Notice that the `operator[]` member is not included in the generic version.

### *A Point on Design*

So far, you have expended a lot of energy to arrive at a class that is not quite as functional as standard pointers. Now that you have the basic pointer class built, however, a couple of things should be apparent. First, you can return to using built-in pointers simply by redeclaring the macros:

```
#define Ptr(T)          T *
#define DeclPtr(T)      /* empty */
```

This works without rewriting a single line of the source code that uses the pointer class.

Second, you have managed to capture every pointer operation that is done on one of our pointer class objects so that they go through a function, which gives you an opportunity to verify those operations by putting together a safe version of the `Pointer` class. The pointer class can also be used to know when objects may safely be reclaimed.

Some environments do not provide a check for operations done on null pointers. Given the pointer class, it is easy to implement such a check:

```
#define MakePtr(T)                                    \
    friend delete(Ptr(T)&)                            \
class Ptr(T) {                                        \
    /* ... */                                         \
    T *operator->()                                   \
      { assert(_ptr); return _ptr; };                 \
    T& operator*()                                    \
      { assert(_ptr); return *_ptr; };                \
    /* ... */                                         \
} ;
```

## 13.5   Reference Counting

One of the uses of a pointer class can be used is for reference-counted objects. Sometimes it is useful to make sure that an object exists as long as there is any reference to it, and that it is deleted when the last reference goes away. If you are willing to accept the weaker guarantee that an object exists so long as there is a counted pointer to it, reference counted garbage-collection can be implemented.

To implement reference counting, two things need to be done. First, the object that will be counted needs to have a member where the count is kept. Second, the pointer class needs to know how to get to this member. This suggests implementing reference counting with a base class:

```
class Counted {
    friend class RPtr;
    int nreferences;     // number of references to this object
    addRef()
        { nreferences++; }
    delRef()
        {
            if (--nreferences)
                delete this;
        }
  public:
    Counted()
        { nreferences = 0; }
    ~Counted();
} ;
```

Any object that needs to be reference counted is derived (possibly indirectly) from this class. Note that the destructor is virtual. This guarantees that the derived class is properly deallocated when the object goes away.

The reference-counted pointer needs to know about the `Counted` class in order to actually do the reference counting. A basic implementation might be:

```
class RPtr {
    Counted *ptr;
  public:
    RPtr()
        { ptr = 0; }
    RPtr(RPtr& r)
        { ptr = r.ptr;
          if(ptr) ptr->addref();
          return *this;
        }
    RPtr(Counted *tp)
        { ptr - tp;
          if(ptr) ptr->addref();
          return *this;
        }
    ~RPtr()
        { if (ptr)  ptr->delref(); }
```

```
RPtr& operator=(RPtr& r)
    { if (ptr) ptr->delref();
      ptr = r.ptr;
      if(ptr) ptr->addref();
      return *this;
    }
RPtr& operator=(Counted *tp)
    { if (ptr) ptr->delref();
      ptr = tp;
      if(ptr) ptr->addref();
      return *this;
    }

Counted& operator *()
    { assert(ptr); return *ptr; }
Counted *operator->()
    { assert(ptr); return ptr; }

operator Counted *()
    { return ptr; }
int operator !()
    { return !ptr; }
} ;
```

Notice that most of the operators defined are identical to the ones for the
base pointer class. The major changes are in assignment and construction.

### *Making* RPtr *Generic*

The biggest problem with the reference counting pointer class is that it
acts like a pointer to Counted rather than like a pointer to the derived
class. On the other hand, you don't want to make a special version of
Counted for each object type, so it is useful to have a base version of the
pointer class that is the friend class known to Counted. A final problem is
making sure that counted pointers can only be defined for types that are
derived from Counted.

The solution lies in creating two classes. RPtr_base is the generic base
class that is common to all counted pointers and is a friend class to
Counted. The derived class implements the actual pointer semantics:

```
class RPtr_base {
  protected:
    Counted *ptr;
    RPtr_base()
        { ptr = 0; }
    RPtr(RPtr& r)
        { ptr = r.ptr;
          if(ptr) ptr->addref();
          return *this;
        }
    RPtr(Counted *tp)
        { ptr = tp;
          if(ptr) ptr->addref();
          return *this;
        }
    ~RPtr()
        { if (ptr)  ptr->delref(); }

    RPtr& operator=(RPtr& r)
        { if (ptr) ptr->delref();
          ptr = r.ptr;
          if(ptr) ptr->addref();
          return *this;
        }
    RPtr& operator=(Counted *tp)
        { if (ptr) ptr->delref();
          ptr = tp;
          if(ptr) ptr->addref();
          return *this;
        }
} ;
```

Notice that everything in the class is protected, including the constructor.
This means that the `RPtr_base` class can only exist as part of a derived
class.  The actual pointer class construction macro is:

```
#define RPtr(T) name2(Rptr_,T)

#define MakeRPtr(T)                                          \
class RPtr(T) : public RPtr_base {                           \
    Counted *ptr;                                            \
  public:                                                    \
    RPtr(T)()                                                \
        : RPtr_base()                                        \
        { }                                                  \
    RPtr(T)(RPtr(T)& r)                                      \
        : RPtr_base(r)                                       \
        { }                                                  \
```

```
    RPtr(T)(T *tp)                                      \
        : RPtr_base((Counted *) T)                      \
        { }                                             \
    ~RPtr(T)()                                          \
        { }                                             \
                                                        \
    RPtr(T)& operator=(RPtr(T)& r)                      \
        { *((RPtr_base *) this) = r; }                  \
    RPtr(T)& operator=(T *tp)                           \
        { *((RPtr_base *) this) =                       \
              (Counted *) tp; }                         \
                                                        \
    T& operator *()                                     \
        { assert(ptr); return *((T *) ptr); }           \
    T *operator->()                                     \
        { assert(ptr); return (T *) ptr; }              \
                                                        \
    operator T *()                                      \
        { return (T *) ptr; }                           \
    int operator !()                                    \
        { return !ptr; }                                \
    } ;
```

The class definition takes advantage of a subtle trick: it is always legal to cast one pointer type to another. Because of this, the code compiles even when the definition for T hasn't been seen. If T is not in fact derived from Counted, the consequences may be difficult to predict. It might be a better choice to omit the casts within the macro and require that T already be defined when the macro is created.

## Exercises

1. C++ defines the arrow operator to be "non-consuming," which means that it may be applied more than once in getting to a member. How is the behavior of

   ```
   (*something).member
   ```

   different from the behavior of

   ```
   something->member?
   ```

2. One of the problems with C++ identified in this chapter is the problem with `operator++`. Suggest a way of differentiating prefix and postfix `++` that is compatible with current usage. What should the rules be for inheriting these operators?

3. One of the ways that a pointer class can be helpful is in detecting use of pointers to objects that have been deleted. Design a mechanism for detecting when a stale pointer references a deleted object.

4. Why is it important that the pointer class be able to convert itself to a real pointer? What caveats need to be understood about using this capability?

5. Is the pointer class a sufficient mechanism for implementing a software paging system? Why or why not?

6. The inline assignment operator is fairly long. Why was inlining this function a good choice in spite of its length?

*All naming problems can be solved by an additional level of indirection.*
*— Anonymous*

# 14

## Atoms

Interpreters raise some interesting problems in string handling that C++ is good at handling. Suppose you are interested in writing an interpreter. It will examine the text of a program and attempt to execute it. For each variable in the program, it is necessary to remember the variable's name so that we can look up the variable's value when you execute the program.

The obvious way to do this is as follows:

1. read a line of input into a buffer,

2. scan for a name,

3. allocate enough space to hold the name,

4. copy the name into the heap.

Variable names, and certainly keywords, tend to be used often, so this strategy is very wasteful. For example, how many times has the keyword `this` been used in this book? If the interpreter isn't clever, it spends a lot of time allocating and deallocating memory to hold these names, many of which are redundant. It also spends a tremendous amount of time in `strcmp()` comparing strings to see if they are equal.

Atoms provide a way to simultaneously reduce string storage space and string comparison time. An atom is a unique 32-bit number that represents the string and is used in its place. No two distinct strings have the same atom associated with them. Every string has exactly one atom. This means that a 32 bit comparison is sufficient to determine string equality.

When a name is first seen by the interpreter, it is interned. This means that the interpreter looks up the string in the list of known atoms, and if it finds it, uses the previously assigned atom value. If the string is not found, a new atom is created. This chapter describes an implementation of atoms and interning in C++. The class is called `NameSpace`.

## 14.1   Constraints

Several constraints need to be met by the implementation. First, it must be cheap to get from an atom to the associated string. Second, it must be cheap to see if a string is already in the table. There isn't an obvious data structure that satisfies both of these needs, which suggests that a hybrid may be in order.

There are a potentially arbitrary number of strings in the world. Because atom values have to be unique, it isn't possible to invent a function that maps each of these strings to a unique 32 bit integer. This suggests that atom values are most easily generated by simply allocating them sequentially. The first atom value is 1, the second 2, and so on.

Why shouldn't you start with 0 as the first atom number? Primarily because it is useful to have a predefined atom which represents the null atom. This serves many of the same purposes as passing a null pointer in place of a string in C++. The obvious value to assign to this atom is 0, which means that other atom values can be allocated starting at 1; incrementing for each new atom.

If atom values are allocated this way, the decision about how to translate the atom value back into the string is pretty straightforward. An array of pointers to the strings is the fastest and most compact representation. The `NameSpace` class is:

```
typedef unsigned long Atom;
const Atom NullAtom = 0;

class NameSpace {
    Atom nextAtomValue;
    BinaryTree nodes;
    char **stringTable;
    int tableLength;
    void growTable();
public:
    NameSpace();
    ~NameSpace();

    Atom intern(char *);
    Atom lookup(char *);
    char *atomName(Atom);
} ;
```

The individual nodes in the binary tree need to hold both the string value and the atom value, so you can make use of the trick mentioned at the end of the `BinaryTree` chapter:

```
struct StringNode {
    int signature;
    char *string;
} ;

struct AtomNode : public StringNode {
    Atom atomValue;
} ;
```

The comparison routine is:

```
static int
CompareAtomStrings(void *v1, void *v2)
{
    StringNode *s1 = (StringNode *) v1;
    StringNode *s2 = (StringNode *) v2;

    if (s1->signature != s2->signature)
        return s1->signature - s2->signature;
    return strcmp(s1->string, s2->string);
}
```

### Construction

Rather than having to allocate the string table from scratch each time, it makes some sense to have a default initial table size. The constructor creates this default-sized table when a `NameSpace` is created.   The insertion routine grows it as needed:

```
NameSpace::NameSpace()
    : nodes(CompareAtomStrings)
{
    tableLength = 128;
    stringTable = new char *[128];
    stringTable[NullAtom] = 0;
}
```

The constructor uses a feature that is seldom needed, but can be very helpful:   the ability to initialize a member with a non-default set of arguments.  The line that reads

```
    : nodes(CompareAtomStrings)
```

says that the `BinaryTree` member should be initialized using the `CompareAtomStrings()` function as its constructor argument.

### Insertion

Inserting a new element into a `NameSpace` involves a couple of steps. First, the incoming string must be turned into an `AtomNode`, and then it must be inserted into the table:

```
Atom
NameSpace::intern(char *s)
{
    AtomNode *anp = new AtomNode;
    AtomNode *oldanp;

    anp->signature = StringSignature(s);
    anp->string = s;

    oldanp = (AtomNode *) nodes.insert(anp);
    if (oldanp != anp) {
        delete anp;
        return oldanp->atomValue;
    }
```

```
    anp->atomValue = nextAtomValue++;
    if (anp->atomValue >= tableLength)
        growTable();

    char * str = new char[strlen(s)+1];
    strcpy(str, s);

    stringTable[anp->atomValue] = str;
    return anp->atomValue;
}
```

The `growTable()` routine simply doubles the size of the existing table:

```
void
NameSpace::growTable()
{
    int newTableLength = 2 * tableLength;
    char **newTable = new char *[newTableLength];
    for (int i = 0; i < tableLength; i++)
        newTable[i] = stringTable[i];
    delete stringTable;
    stringTable = newTable;
}
```

## *Looking Atoms Up*

Looking up a string by name isn't quite as complicated as inserting one:

```
Atom
NameSpace::lookup(char *s)
{
    AtomNode *anp;
    StringNode sn;

    sn.signature = StringSignature(s);
    sn.string = s;

    anp = (AtomNode *) nodes.lookup(&sn);

    if (anp)
        return anp->atomValue;

    return NullAtom;
}
```

The conversion from an atom value to the actual string is of course trivial:

```
char *
NameSpace::atomName(Atom atom)
{
    return stringTable[atom];
}
```

## 14.2  Implementation Deficiencies

While this version of the `NameSpace` class is complete and functional, it isn't very good.  An atom manager tends to be a performance-critical piece of code for programs that use it, and the implementation that I have given does too many memory allocations to be considered a good one.

There is a more important flaw, however, which is that the search code probably shouldn't be based on a binary tree at all.  A binary tree is an acceptable implementation for handling tens of atoms, but is probably not a good choice for a compiler or any other program that needs to handle hundreds or thousands of atoms.  For such applications, a hash table is a better choice.

The new declaration for `NameSpace` is not much more complicated than the previous one:

```
typedef unsigned char CharPtr;
MakeHashTable(CharPtr);

class NameSpace {
    Atom nextAtomValue;
    HashTable(CharPtr) nodes;
    char *stringTable;
    int tableLength;
    void growTable();
public:
    NameSpace();
    ~NameSpace();

    Atom intern(char *);
    Atom lookup(char *);
    char *atomName(Atom);
} ;
```

The implementation, however, is a little bit more work.  Before doing the complicated part, let's deal with the parts that don't change much:

```
NameSpace::NameSpace()
    : nodes(strcmp)
{
    tableLength = 128;
    stringTable = new char *[128];
    stringTable[NullAtom] = 0;
}

void
NameSpace::growTable()
{
    int newTableLength = 2 * tableLength;
    char **newTable = new char *[newTableLength];
    for (int i = 0; i < tableLength; i++)
        newTable[i] = stringTable[i];
    delete stringTable;
    stringTable = newTable;
}

char *
NameSpace::atomName(Atom atom)
{
    return stringTable[atom];
}
```

## The lookup routine is greatly simplified:

```
Atom
NameSpace::lookup(char *s)
{
    // Since HashTable::lookup returns 0 on not found,
    // that case converts to NullAtom, which is what we want.
    Atom a = (Atom) nodes.lookup(s);
}
```

## As is the insertion routine:

```
Atom
NameSpace::intern(char *s)
{
    // Since HashTable::lookup returns 0 on not found,
    // that case converts to NullAtom, which is what we want.
    Atom a = (Atom) nodes.lookup(s);

    if (a != NullAtom)
        return a;

    a = nextAtomValue++;
```

```
        if (a >= tableLength)
            growTable();

        char * str = new char[strlen(s)+1];
        strcpy(str, s);

        nodes.add(str, (void *) a);
        return a;
    }
```

## Building the Hash Algorithm

So much for the easy part. The question that remains is: what to do about a hash routine? Many computer systems have an online dictionary of some form. Typically, these have a fairly well-developed list of words in them, so they are an ideal source of test material for a hash algorithm. Out of curiosity, the first algorithm I tried was the original signature algorithm. Since the algorithm was already handy, I was reluctant to throw it away without considering it. For 4096 buckets it proves to be an excellent hash algorithm:

```
int
HashTable(CharPtr)::hash(register CharPtr key)
{
    int i;
    int len = strlen(key);
    unsigned signature = 0;

    for (i = 0; i < (len+1)/2; i++)
    {
        signature = signature * 27 + key[i];
        signature = signature * 27 + key[len - 1 - i];
    }

    return signature % NBUCKETS;
}
```

The UNIX spelling dictionary on my system has 23,784 words in it. To test out the hash algorithm, I ran it against all of the strings for successively smaller bucket sizes. The distribution of items over 4096 buckets is nearly perfect. The biggest bucket holds 16 items while the average bucket holds only 6. This means that the hash table based version does a little less than half the work of the binary tree version.

## Exercises

1.  It should be clear that the `NameSpace` class could be implemented using either binary trees or hash tables. Are hash tables always a better choice? What determines which choice is better?

2.  A problem with the `NameSpace` class is that if there is more than one namespace instance the same atom value can mean different things in different namespaces. Suggest a one line change to `NameSpace` that eliminates this problem.

3.  Occasionally, you will really need to maintain two distinct name spaces, as when a client connects to multiple servers. How can `NameSpace` be changed to handle this problem? What is the cost of doing so?

4.  A problem with the `NameSpace` class is that you can never throw an old name away. The `NameSpace` design guarantees that once an atom is assigned to a string, it remains valid forever. How often is this a problem in practice? When it is a problem, suggest an alternative method for string management that might be more appropriate.

*In the beginning was the word, all right —*
*but it wasn't a fixed number of bits!*
                                    *— R. Barton*

# 15

# Memory Management

Indirection is one of the principle implementation tools for abstraction. The HashTable implementation depended on being able to use pointers to the actual objects to avoid needing to know what they were. The string version of the BinaryTree implementation used an internally allocated structure. It contained a pointer to the real string and a signature to hide the implementation logic from the user and present a familiar interface. Both allocated internal structure dynamically to implement the supporting structures for fast search.

C++ programs, much more than C programs, take advantage of the heap. As a result, C++ objects are more frequently allocated in the heap than their C counterparts. Careful memory management is a crucial aspect of C++ performance. As compilers get better, it will very likely become the dominant issue in tuning C++ applications.

In release 2.0 of the C++ language, two new operators were introduced to allow programmers to have better control over heap allocation. These operators are the new and delete operators. This chapter discusses some techniques for deciding how and when to take advantage of these operators.

## Traditional Memory Management

Consider an application that builds a hash table of 16,000 entries or so. For each of these entries, a hash table data structure gets allocated in the heap:

```
struct HashEntry {
    unsigned long key;      /* hash key */
    void          *value;
    HashEntry     *next, *prev;

    HashEntry(unsigned long newkey)
        { key = newkey; next = 0; prev = 0; }
    ~HashEntry()
        {
            if (next) next->prev = prev;
            if (prev) prev->next = next;
        }
} ;
```

Traditional heap allocation schemes use a first fit strategy for finding a new chunk of memory when it is needed. The memory allocators walk through the memory free list trying to locate a block big enough to hold what you want. If none is available, they allocate a new one.

The problem with this strategy is what happens when the heap has become fragmented. In this case, the first fit algorithm will walk through essentially every page in the heap before concluding that the heap needs to grow, which has awful performance consequences.

One technique for improving this is to allocate memory in sizes that are a multiple of two. If you allocate a 43 byte structure, the memory management system returns a 64 byte structure. Free memory is kept in a table that is indexed by size. When hunting for a new block, the system is able to avoid walking through any blocks that are too small. If a block of the appropriate size cannot be found, the memory manager breaks a block of the next larger size into two smaller blocks and gives one to the user.

This strategy has its own problems, however. When memory is freed, it must be put on the correct list for reallocation, which means that it carries around with it a word that describes its size. Since this word is part of the allocated region, it is added to the size for which you ask. As a result, asking for a chunk of memory whose size is a power of two is pathological; you always get a chunk that is the next larger power of two, effectively doubling the amount of memory your application needs. Notice that the hash table node structure size is a power of two on most systems (32 bytes). Our 16,000 nodes suddenly take a megabyte to store instead of half a megabyte.

## 15.1   The C++ Solution: Operators `new()` and `delete()`

Operators `new()` and `delete()` were invented to address the need for more precise memory management. Because you know the types of the objects that are being allocated and deallocated, you can do very efficient storage management on a per-object-type basis, so long as there are hooks into the memory management system. `New` and `delete` provide these hooks.

Each of these operators has two variants. The first is passed the size of the desired object. The second is passed the size and the location at which the object should be placed. It is intended for use in arena management.

Suppose you are interested in speeding the allocation of hash table nodes. An obvious thing to do is to arrange to allocate some large number of them up front from the system's memory manager, and dole them out as you need them:

```
static HashEntry *nextFree = 0
static HashEntry *notFree = 0;

void *
HashEntry::operator new(size_t size)
{
    if (size != sizeof(*this))   // user is playing heap games

        return ::new(size);
    if (notFree == nextFree) {
        nextFree = (HashEntry *) new(sizeof(*this) * 1024);

        notFree = nextFree + 1024;
    }

    return nextFree++;
}
```

This version of the `new()` operator doesn't do any heap walking at all. It is about as efficient as such a routine can get. If you trust the user, the check for heap games can be eliminated, but it isn't very expensive.

Note, however, that this version of the `new()` operator doesn't attempt to reuse freed blocks. In order to ensure that freed blocks do not get handed back to the global memory manager for reallocation, an operator `delete()` must be defined:

```
void *
HashEntry::operator delete(void *object)
{
    // don't ever free storage for these!
}
```

I have seen performance differences of a factor of 40 between applications that do not use this sort of technique and those that do. Its effect is most dramatic when you never intend to free the objects.

The advantage to having the `new()` and `delete()` operators be accessable for redefinition is that this tuning can, to a large degree, be done after the implementation is completed.

### When Objects Are Reused

Similar performance advantages can be attained when objects need to be reused. The strategy is much the same as the strategy used by the standard memory management software, but it is able to improve the locality of reference by making many objects share the same pages in memory:

```
static HashEntry *nextFree = 0
static HashEntry *notFree = 0;
static HashEntry *deleteChain = 0;

void *
HashEntry::operator new(size_t size)
{
    if (size != sizeof(*this))   // user is playing heap games
        return ::new(size);
```

```
        // see if one was deleted
        if (deleteChain) {
            HashEntry *obj = deleteChain;
            deleteChain = *((HashEntry **) deleteChain);
            return obj;
        }

        // otherwise take the next one from the allocation block
        if (notFree == nextFree) {
            nextFree = (HashEntry *) new(sizeof(*this) * 1024);
            notFree = nextFree + 1024;
        }

        return nextFree++;
    }
```

In this version, the `delete()` operator places newly deleted objects onto a linked list:

```
void *
HashEntry::operator delete(void *object)
{
    HashEntry **hep = (HashEntry **) object;
    *hep = deleteChain;
    deleteChain = this;
}
```

Note that the `delete()` operators might not capture all of the objects that were allocated by the `new()` operators. In particular, the following code sequence will allocate an object using `HashEntry::new()` but deallocate it using the global `delete()` operator:

```
void * v = new HashEntry;
// ... some intervening code...
delete v;
```

This can cause some interesting surprises. Operators `new()` and `delete()` should therefore be used sparingly.

### *Forcing Construction and Destruction*

One of the useful attributes of the `new()` and `delete()` operators is that they can be used to force in-place construction and deletion to happen. This is especially useful when trying to grow or shrink an array.

For example, suppose you have allocated an array of 16 items in the heap and wish to grow it to an array of 32 items.  Because the first 16 items have already been constructed, you don't want to construct them again. The correct way to do this is to say:

```
Object *newArray = (Object *) new char[sizeof(OBJECT) *32];
new(newArray+16) Object[16];
memcpy(newArray, oldArray, sizeof(Object) * 16);
delete (void *) oldArray;
```

This sequence causes only the second half of the new array to be constructed, and prevents the old array from being destructed.  Because the constructors may be arbitrarily complicated, and the destructors might try to recursively remove things, it is an important condition to watch out for.

The C++ controls over memory management are very simple, and surprisingly versatile.  Using them selectively is well worthwhile.

*If you are worried about sloppiness on-line,*
*make your users pay real money; this helps.*
                                    *— D. Ross*

# 16

# Tuning Performance

It is a continuing source of amazement to me how many teachers and mentors believe that compilers are good at doing performance tuning. I have been hearing various forms of this misleading advice for ten years. If anything, it is less true today than it used to be. Register allocation is easy if you only have two or three registers. Modern architectures have lots of them. The vast majority of compilers in the world have minimal or nonexistant optimizers. The best performance tuning, even in portable code, is still done by human beings.

I should emphasize that this chapter focuses on some very low-level issues. It does not try to set forth the best strategies. Rather, it tries to set forth some guidelines that have proven useful in practice. Beyond a certain point, the gains to be had from hand-tuned performance are minimal. The best strategy for finding critical paths in the code is to use profiling tools and tune only the code that needs it. What this chapter does focus on is the techniques that you can use as you write the code to prevent it from being capriciously butchered by stupid compilers.

C++ provides three tools for helping the compiler generate good code. These are the `register` keyword, the `inline` keyword, and the call-by-reference syntax.

## 16.1   **Using** `inline`

Of the three performance tuning facilities, the `inline` keyword is the most difficult to understand. Whether you want a procedure to be inlined depends on the complexity of the code, the frequency with which it is called, the cost of doing procedure calls on your machine, and the intelligence of the optimizer.

### *Trivial Cases*

In some cases, it is trivially obvious that inlining a function is the right thing to do. The most common examples of this are accessors and mutators:

```
SomeClass::state()
{
    return _state;
}

SomeClass::setState(State state)
{
    _state = state;
}
```

Procedures like these almost always want to be inlined. Indeed, it is essential to good code generation that they are, because the vast majority of compilers won't inline them automatically.

More to the point, the inlined code in these cases tends to generate about two instructions, instead of the eight to ten required for a typical procedure call. Inlining these functions is a win, and I have tried to do so consistently throughout the book. Including a member function implementation in a class declaration causes it to be inlined.

Array indexing to get to the value isn't always as clear cut, but is usually a win. Functions that compute arithmetic operations very often win, as long as they don't do too many operations (about six).

### Conditional Execution

Sometimes a function does exactly one of several operations conditionally, and the condition can be proven by the compiler at the call site:

```
inline int
abs(int i)
{
    return (i < 0) ? -i; i;
}
```

It is very likely that the compiler knows whether or not *i* is negative at the call site. In addition, when tests such as these are integrated into a larger body of code, they can often be folded in with other tests.

A better example of conditional inlining being a win can be found in the memory allocation code from the previous chapter. By inlining the `new` operator, the compiler can eliminate most of the function call overhead of memory allocation.

### Loops

Tight loops might seem to be good choices for inlining. In some cases, the entire loop would take up no more code than the function call if it were inlined. This is especially true of initialization code:

```
void
initialize()
{
    for(int i = 0; i < 1024; i++)
        x[i] = i;
}
```

Unfortunately, implementations of C++ based on the *cfront* translator from AT&T are not able to inline loops.

### Other Cases

Most of the cases where inlining is of real performance benefit have to do with inner loops, where an optimizer can schedule code inside a loop that was previously hidden by an out-of-line procedure call. Until C++

implementations handle inlining of loops, these cases aren't helped much by the `inline` keyword. If you have any doubts, *don't inline!*

## 16.2   Register Allocation

In principle, register allocation should be extremely sensitive to the type of machine on which your code is running. In practice, it often isn't, because real programs tend to run on a pretty homogeneous set of machines. A program designed to run on a 10 MIPS workstation probably doesn't need to worry about running on an 8086 microprocessor, though it may need to run on the 80386. Similarly, a program designed to run on a 6502 isn't likely to care about the register properties of the 68000 series. There are many exceptions, but it is surprising how much benefit can be obtained with a simple model for register allocation.

### *How Many Registers?*

Most processors have somewhere between three and six registers available for allocation in each procedures. Those processors that have more frequently divide them into local and global registers or into register windows. Compilers for these processors tend to need to do sophisticated register allocation that is not in any way inhibited by the strategy suggested here.

Let's take a piece of code with six register declarations:

```
{
    register int r1;
    register int r2;
    register int r3;
    register int r4;
    register int r5;
    register int r6;
}
```

If the compiler pays attention to the user's register hints at all, it usually assigns registers in sequence until it runs out. On a machine with three per procedure registers, *r1* through *r3* will end up in registers. On a machine with six available registers, all of the variables will be assigned to registers. I tend to use the working assumption that there are six registers available to me.

This suggests a first rule for using the `register` keyword: Put the most important variables first.

### Important Variables

The question then becomes: What is an important variable? Are there any variables that *don't* want to be in registers?

Perhaps surprisingly, the answer is yes: some variables do not want to be in registers. Each register that is used in a procedure has to be saved on procedure entry and restored when the procedure exits. This requires two instructions, plus a third to initialize the register if it needs to be initialized. If a variable is used less than three times, it doesn't pay to do all of this overhead. The program will spend more time saving and restoring the register than it will get back by having the value in a register.

This gives us a second rule of thumb: If you don't use it at least three times, don't put it in a register.

Variables that are used inside of loops should be counted as being used as many times as you think the loop will be executed *on average*. Most optimizers arbitrarily decide that every usage of a variable inside a loop should be multiplied by ten when deciding which variables should go into registers.

Array base addresses and pointers into the heap that are heavily used inside a loop are good candidates for registers, as are variables that are passed to procedures often.

### Using Scopes Effectively

Even on a machine that has a good optimizer, there is considerable benefit to making careful use of scopes. Consider the problem of allocating registers to the following function:

```
MyFunction()
{
    register int i;
    register int j;

        for(i = 0; i < 10; i++) {
            // ... do something not involving j ...
        }
    }

    {

        register int j;
        for (j = 0; j < 100; j++) {
            // ... do something not involving i...
        }
    }
}
```

Because of the placement of the declarations, the programmer has asserted that both i and j are alive throughout the whole function. If there are four or five other variables assigned to registers, many compilers would exclude one or the other variable from a register, even though they can be assigned to the same register. A better version of the function would make it clear that the two variables are independent by making use of scopes:

```
MyFunction()
{
    {

        register int i;

        for(i = 0; i < 10; i++) {
            // ... do something not involving j ...
        }
    }

    {

        register int j;
        for (j = 0; j < 100; j++) {
            // ... do something not involving i...
        }
    }
}
```

Even a simple compiler will allocate both of these variables to registers. Figuring out where a variable is really used in a function is one of the more difficult parts of writing register allocation algorithms. Proper use of scopes can make a tremendous difference in the performance of your programs.

*Summary*

The model for doing register allocation that I have described here works well in practice. It is simple enough that it can be used as a matter of course in writing your code. It makes few enough assumptions that you are not likely to get bad code out of a good optimizer by using it. On those compilers that don't do register allocation well it can make a big difference.

There are some who argue that register allocation is the compilers job. More importantly, they are arguing that the amount of time you will spend tuning your code at this level is more effort than it is worth. That is why the model is simple. It has to be simple to be worth using.

At the very least, make sure to put in the register declarations on those procedures where your program spends a lot of time.

## 16.3 Passing by Reference

Another tool that helps application performance is to pass objects by reference whenever possible. Instead of copying the whole object onto the stack, passing objects by reference simply passes the object pointer. If the recipient doesn't modify the object in any case, no harm is done, and no source code changes need to be made to change the calling convention.

Once the `const` keyword problems in the language have been resolved, you might think about declaring your procedures to take a constant reference, which will get the compiler to help you ensure that you don't modify the object.

*Languages form our thinking habits... and I think it is fair to say that many of the problems plaguing the world of software are more or less directly attributable to the rather poor present state of language development.*

*— N. Wirth*

# Templates

Implementing generic classes with the C preprocessor is painful. The preprocessor suffers from several limitations that are difficult to manage. For example, you can't declare a variable-length array of strings by writing

```
MakeVarArray(char *);
```

using the preprocessor mechanism. Instead, you must introduce a type definition to work around the naming problem:

```
typedef char *charPtr;
MakeVarArray(charPtr);
```

Creating such a type definition isn't a bad thing *per se*, but you shouldn't be forced to do so because of an inadequate parameterization mechanism.

Classes built with macros also suffer from debugging problems. If the macro proves to be wrong, line number information is essentially useless. As a result, building correct parameterized classes can be very difficult.

On the other hand, parameterized classes are essential for writing reusable code. The Array class would be considerably less useful if each time you built one you needed to cut and paste the original implementation and modify it for use with a new type. The good news is that C++ has a better mechanism.  The bad news is that it isn't likely to be implemented in the immediate future.

The *C++ 2.0 Reference Manual* has two undefined chapters in it that are place holders for the forthcoming templates and exception handling features.  The templates mechanism provides a way to build generic classes within the language.  This chapter briefly describes the latest version of the templates proposal, and shows how to implement a few of the generic classes with it.  It seems appropriate to emphasize that the code is very likely wrong.  The templates mechanism is still in the working proposal stage.  Because there is no implementation, it's hard to test the code.

A paper describing the templates proposal can be found in the Proceedings of the 1988 USENIX C++ Conference.  Copies of the proceedings can be obtained from the USENIX Association, P.O. Box 2299, Berkeley, California, 94710.

## 17.1  Templates

Template definitions are introduced by the `template` keyword.  A template describes a generic form of a class that will be expanded as needed by the compiler when the class is used.  For example, the generic pointer class might be written as:

```
template <class T> class Ptr {
    T *ptr;
  public:
    Ptr()
      { ptr = 0; }
    Ptr(Ptr& r)
      { ptr = r.ptr; }
    Ptr(T *p)
      { ptr = p; }
    ~Ptr()
      { }

    operator T *()
      { return ptr; }
    T *operator->()
      { return ptr; }
```

```
    T& operator*()
        { return *ptr; }
    T& operator[](int);
} ;
```

The `template` keyword can be used to define a parameterized function or class. The objects named within the angle braces describe how the definition is parameterized. The `class` keyword indicates that the definition is parameterized over a type.

A template definition doesn't actually define any types. After the template has been seen you can write:

```
Ptr<int> pi;
Ptr<float> pf;
```

When the compiler sees the first use of such a type, it uses the template to generate the type automatically. You can think of the process as operating just like the preprocessor macro expansion. When the compiler sees the use of `Ptr<int>`, it generates:

```
class Ptr_int {
    int *ptr;
  public:
    Ptr_int()
        { ptr = 0; }
    Ptr_int(Ptr_int& r)
        { ptr = r.ptr; }
    Ptr_int(int *p)
        { ptr = p; }
    ~Ptr_int()
        { }

    operator int *()
        { return ptr; }
    int *operator->()
        { return ptr; }
    int& operator*()
        { return *ptr; }
    int& operator[](int);
} ;
```

Because the templates mechanism is part of the language, the type can be arbitrary. There is no need to limit yourself to an identifier. The definitions

```
Ptr<char *> ppc
Ptr<int (*)(const char *, ...)> ppf;
```

define a `Ptr` to pointer to characters and a `Ptr` to pointer to function, respectively.

The templates mechanism can also be used to define functions:

```
template <class T> T& Ptr<T>::operator[](int i)
{
    return ptr[i];
}

template <class T> int compare(T, T);

int compare<char>(char a, char b)
{
    return b - a;
}
```

Notice that a template can be used to define the general form of the function while the actual implementation is managed on a case-by-case basis by the user. The compiler does not attempt to automatically generate the needed functions. This allows the user to implement efficient versions of the routine for types that have special implementations. The template can be used to generate the other versions by using a special mode of the compiler.

## 17.2   Parameterizing Over Variables and Constants

Another useful kind of parameterization, and one that is often ignored, is parameterizing over variables. As an example, consider a technique that could prove very useful for error handling:

```
template <int fatal(const char *,...) = GlobalFatal>
class Lexer {
    // ... Contents of a Lexer ...
    handleError()
      { fatal("This is error number %d\n", 10); }
} ;
```

The version of the fatal routine to be called can be defined when the lexer is instantiated:

```
Lexer<fatal1> lexer1;
Lexer<fatal2> lexer2;
```

If no error handler is supplied, the error handler defaults to `GlobalFatal`:

```
Lexer lexerUsingGlobalFatal;
```

One might also contemplate defining a queue of some fixed number of elements, all of which are of type `T`:

```
template <class T, int N> class Queue {
    T queueEntries[N];
    int queueDepth;
  public:
    // .... rest of Queue class...
} ;
```

Each of these cases makes the parameterization more general.

## 17.3  Building the Array Classes with Templates

To explore another example of how templates are used, the generic array classes are very easy to build with the templates mechnanism. The `Array` class is defined by:

```
template <class T>
class Array {
 protected:
    int _sz;
    int _needsFree;
    T *_contents;

 public:
    Array(int sz, int zeroed = 1)
        {
            _contents = sz ? new T[sz] : 0;
            _needsFree = 1;
            _sz = sz;
            if (zeroed) memset(_contents, 0, sizeof(T)*sz);
        }
```

```
Array(T *staticArray, int numElements)
    {
        _needsFree = 0;
        _contents = staticArray;
        _sz = numElements;
    }

~Array()
    { if (_needsFree)
        delete _contents; }

T& operator[](int i)
    { return _contents[i]; }

operator T *()
    { return _contents; }

int size()
    { return sizeof(T) * _sz; }
} ;
```

The variable length array class can then be derived from the generic `Array` class:

```
#include <assert.h>

temnplate <class T>
class DynamicArray : public Array<T> {
 protected:
    void grow(int newSize);
 public:
    DynamicArray()
    : Array()
        { }

    DynamicArray(int sz)
    : Array(sz)
        { }

    ~DynamicArray();

    T& operator[](int i)
        {
            if(i >= sz)
                grow(i);
            return _contents[i];
        }
} ;
```

```
#define GROWRATE 1024

template <class T>
void
DynamicArray::grow(int ndx)
{
  register void *oldContents = _contents;
  register int oldSz = _sz;
  register T *newBuf;

  while (_sz <= ndx)
    _sz += GROWRATE;

  register int nbytes = _sz * sizeof(T);
  newBuf = (T *) new char[nbytes];

  if(oldContents)
    memcpy(newBuf, oldContents, oldSz * sizeof(T));

  delete oldContents;

  /* now arrange for the new ones to get initialized:   */

  new(newBuf + oldSz) T[_sz - oldSz];
  _contents = (T *) newBuf;
}
```

As you can see, the implementation isn't substantially different from the one in the "Dynamic Arrays" chapter, but it is considerably cleaner and has a reasonable chance of continuing to work over time.

One of the goals in deciding how to use the preprocessor was to arrive at a mechanism that would not require user code to be changed when templates are implemented. Once a templates version of the pointer class has been defined, for example, the macro can be changed to read

```
#define Ptr(T) Ptr<T>
```

Existing code will then continue to work transparently with the new definition.

# Complete Classes

The following pages contain complete listings for the classes described in *A C++ Toolkit*. They are collected here for your examination and use.

You may use and redistribute the programs and code fragments in this book without royaltee or fee, provided that the following notice is included in the associated documentation and in the online program information display:

## SimpleString Definition

```
// SimpleString class.
// This class demonstrates the use of construction,
// initialization, and operator overloading.
//
// This class is not a complete String implementation by any
// stretch of the imagination.

#include <string.h>

class SimpleString {
    char *_string;
    int _length;
  public:
    SimpleString();
    SimpleString(const char*);
    SimpleString::SimpleString(SimpleString& s);
    ~SimpleString();

    const char *string() const;
    SimpleString& operator=(const char *);
    SimpleString& operator=(const SimpleString&);
} ;
```

## SimpleString Implementation

```
char *
Strdup(const char *s)
{
    char *s2 = new char[strlen(s) + 1];
    strcpy(s2, s);

    return s2;
}

SimpleString::SimpleString()
{
    _string = 0;
    _length = 0;
}

SimpleString::~SimpleString()
{
    delete _string;
}

SimpleString::SimpleString(SimpleString& s)
{
    if (s._string) {
        _string = Strdup(s._string);
        _length = s._length;
    }
    else {
        _string = 0;
        _length = 0;
    }
}

SimpleString::SimpleString(const char * s)
{
    _string = s ? strdup(s) : 0;
    _length = s ? strlen(s) : 0;
}

const char *
SimpleString::string()
const
{
    return _string;
} ;
```

```
SimpleString&
SimpleString::operator=(const char *s)
{
    delete _string;
    _string = s ? strdup(s) : 0;
    _length = s ? strlen(s) : 0;
    return *this;
}

SimpleString&
SimpleString::operator=(const SimpleString& s)
{
    delete _string;
    _string = s._string ? strdup(s._string) : 0;
    _length = _string ? s._length : 0;
    return *this;
}
```

## Point Definition

```
// The point class is principly intended as an example of how
// arithmetic operators are overloaded, and of how a complete
// abstraction can be built as a class

typedef int Coord;

class Point {
    int _xpos, _ypos;
public:
    Point();
    Point(Coord, Coord);
    Point(const Point&);
    ~Point();

    Point operator-(const Point&) const;
    Point operator+(const Point&) const;
    Point operator*(Coord) const;
    Point operator/(Coord) const;

    Point& operator=(const Point&);
    Point& operator-=(const Point&);
    Point& operator+=(const Point&);
    Point& operator*=(Coord);
    Point& operator/=(Coord);

    Coord x() const { return _xpos; }
    Coord y() const { return _ypos; }

    Point& setX(Coord x)
      { _xpos = x; return *this; }
    Point& setY(Coord y)
      { _ypos = y; return *this; }
};
```

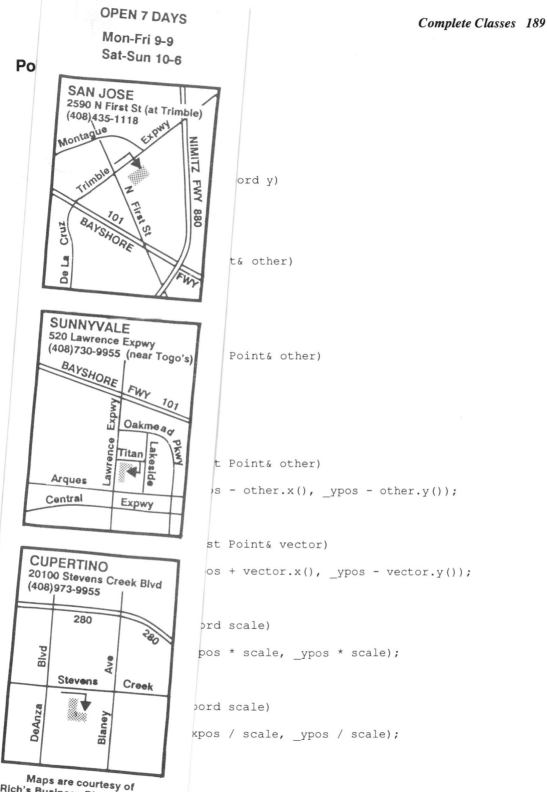

OPEN 7 DAYS
Mon-Fri 9-9
Sat-Sun 10-6

Po

SAN JOSE
2590 N First St (at Trimble)
(408) 435-1118

Montague   Expwy
Trimble
NIMITZ FWY 880
N First St
De La Cruz
101
BAYSHORE
FWY

SUNNYVALE
520 Lawrence Expwy
(408) 730-9955 (near Togo's)

BAYSHORE   FWY   101
Lawrence Expwy
Oakmead Pkwy
Titan
Lakeside
Arques
Central   Expwy

CUPERTINO
20100 Stevens Creek Blvd
(408) 973-9955

280
280
Blvd
Ave
Stevens   Creek
DeAnza
Blaney

Maps are courtesy of
Rich's Business Directories Inc

```
ord y)


t& other)


Point& other)


t Point& other)
os - other.x(), _ypos - other.y());


st Point& vector)
os + vector.x(), _ypos - vector.y());


ord scale)
pos * scale, _ypos * scale);


ord scale)
xpos / scale, _ypos / scale);
```

```
Point&
Point::operator-=(const Point& vector)
{
    _xpos -= vector.x();
    _ypos -= vector.y();
    return *this;
}

Point&
Point::operator+=(const Point& vector)
{
    _xpos += vector.x();
    _ypos += vector.y();
    return *this;
}

Point&
Point::operator*=(Coord scale)
{
    _xpos *= scale;
    _ypos *= scale;
    return *this;
}

Point&
Point::operator/=(Coord scale)
{
    _xpos /= scale;
    _ypos /= scale;
    return *this;
}
```

# Rectangle

```
// The Rectangle class deomstrates how to make use of the
// abstraction implemented by the Point class, including
// all of hte arithmetic operators that were implemented

class Rectangle {
    Point _ll;
    Point _ur;

  public:
    Coord height();
    Coord width();

    Rectangle(const Point& p1, const Point& p2)
      { _ll = p1; _ur = p2; }

    Point lowerLeft()
      const { return _ll; }
    Point upperRight()
      const { return _ur; }

    Point center()
      const { return (_ur + _ll) / 2; }

    Rectangle& moveTo(const Point&);
      { _ur += _ll - where;
        _ur += where;
        return *this;         }
    Rectangle& moveTo(Coord dx, Coord dy);
      { _ll += Point(dx,dy);
        _ur += Point(dx,dy);
        return *this;         }

    Rectangle& setWidth(Coord w)
      { _ur.setX(_ll.x() + w); return *this; }
    Rectangle& setHeight(Coord h)
      { _ur.setY(_ll.y() + h); return *this; }
} ;
```

## Square

```
// The square class demonstrates derivation (aka subclassing).  A
// square is a special case of a rectangle

class Square : public Rectangle {
  public:
    Square(const Point& p1, const Point& p2)
      : Rectangle(p1, Point(p2.x(), p2.x() - p1.x() + p1.x()))
      { }

    Square& moveTo(Point& p)
      { Rectangle::moveTo(p); return *this; }

    Square& setWidth(Coord w)
      { Rectangle::setWidth(w); Rectangle::setHeight(w);
        return *this; }

    Square& setHeight(Coord h)
      { Rectangle::setWidth(h); Rectangle::setHeight(h);
        return *this; }
} ;
```

## GeomObject Definition

```
// GeomObject demonstrates the use of derivation to implement
// factorization.  All geomtric objects have certain operations
// in common.  These are captured by the GeomObject class.

class GeomObject {
  protected:
    struct {
      Point _ll, _ur;   // bounding box
    } _boundingBox;
  public:
    GeomObject(const Point& p1, const Point& p2)
      { _boundingBox._ll = p1; _boundingBox._ur = p2; }
    ~GeomObject()  {};

    Point center()      // return the center of the bounding box
      const { return (_boundingBox._ll + _boundingBox._ur) /2; }
    int intersects(const GeomObject& ob) const;
    int height()
      const { return _boundingBox._ur.y() -
                     _boundingBox._ll.y(); }
    int width()
      const { return _boundingBox._ur.x() -
                     _boundingBox._ll.x(); }
    const Point& upperRight()
      const { return _boundingBox._ur; }
    const Point& lowerLeft()
      const { return _boundingBox._ll; }

    GeomObject& moveTo(const Point& p)
      { _boundingBox._ur += (p - _boundingBox._ll);
        _boundingBox._ll = p; return *this; }

    GeomObject& operator=(const GeomObject& o)
      { _boundingBox._ur = o._boundingBox._ur;
        _boundingBox._ll = o._boundingBox._ll;
        return *this; }

    GeomObject& move(const Point& delta)
      { _boundingBox._ll += delta;
        _boundingBox._ur += delta;
        return *this; }
} ;
```

## GeomObject Implementation

```
int
GeomObject::intersects(const GeomObject& o)
const
{
    if (upperRight().x() < o.lowerLeft().x() ||
        upperRight().y() < o.lowerLeft().y()     ||
        lowerLeft().x() > o.upperRight().x() ||
        lowerLeft().y() > o.upperRight().y())
        return 0;
    return 1;
}
```

## GeomObject-Based Rectangle

```
// This version of the Rectangle class demonstrates how to
// make use of the common base functionality provided by
// GeomObject.

class Rectangle : public GeomObject {
public:
    Rectangle(const Point& p1, const Point& p2)
      : GeomObject(p1, p2)
      { }
    Rectangle(const Rectangle& r)
      : GeomObject(r.lowerLeft(), r.upperRight())
      { }
    Rectangle& operator=(const Rectangle& r)
      { GeomObject::operator=((GeomObject) r); return *this; }

    Rectangle& moveTo(const Point& p);
      { GeomObject::moveTo(p);
        return *this; }
    Rectangle& moveTo(Coord dx, Coord dy);
      { GeomObject::moveTo(Point(dx, dy));
        return *this; }
} ;
```

## Point3d Definition

```
// The Point3d class demonstrates that some problems cannot
// be addressed by subclassing.  Moving from a two-dimensional
// to a three-dimensional coordinate system is a paradigmatic
// shift.

class Point3d {
    int _xpos, _ypos, _zpos;
public:
    Point3d();
    Point3d(Coord, Coord, Coord);
    Point3d(const Point3d&);
    ~Point3d();

    Point3d operator-(const Point3d&) const;
    Point3d operator+(const Point3d&) const;
    Point3d operator*(Coord) const;
    Point3d operator/(Coord) const;

    Point3d& operator=(const Point3d&);
    Point3d& operator-=(const Point3d&);
    Point3d& operator+=(const Point3d&);
    Point3d& operator*=(Coord);
    Point3d& operator/=(Coord);

    Coord x() const;
    Coord y() const;
    Coord z() const;

    Point3d& setX(Coord);
    Point3d& setY(Coord);
    Point3d& setZ(Coord);
} ;
```

## Set256 Definition

```
// Set256 implmements a 256 element set, suitable for use for
// managing a set of ASCII characters, for example.  This is
// the less general form of the generic set class.

class Set256 {
    unsigned long bits[256/(sizeof(unsigned long) * 8)];
public:
    Set256()
        { memset(bits, 0, sizeof(bits)); }
    ~Set256()
        { }

    Set256& clear()
        { memset(bits, 0, sizeof(bits));
          return *this;}
    Set256& fill()
        { memset(bits, ~0, sizeof(bits));
          return *this;}

    // assignment and initialization:
    Set256(Set256& s);
    Set256& operator=(Set256& s);

    // operations on elements:
    Set256 operator &(unsigned u);
    Set256 operator |(unsigned u);
    Set256 operator -(unsigned u);

    // destructive versions:
    Set256& operator &=(unsigned u);
    Set256& operator |=(unsigned u);
    Set256& operator -=(unsigned u);

    // operations on Set256s:
    Set256 operator &(Set256& s);
    Set256 operator |(Set256& s);
    Set256 operator -(Set256& s);

    // destructive versions:
    Set256& operator &=(Set256& s);
    Set256& operator |=(Set256& s);
    Set256& operator -=(Set256& s);
} ;
```

## Set256 Implementation

```
#define ULONG_BITS (sizeof(unsigned long) * 8)

Set256 Set256::operator &(unsigned u)
{
    Set256 newSet(*this);

    newSet &= u;
    return newSet;
}

Set256 Set256::operator |(unsigned u)
{
    Set256 newSet(*this);

    newSet |= u;
    return newSet;
}

Set256 Set256::operator -(unsigned u)
{
    Set256 newSet(*this);

    newSet -= u;
    return newSet;
}

Set256& Set256::operator &=(unsigned u)
{
    bits[u/32] &= (u+1) % 32;
    return *this;
}

Set256& Set256::operator |=(unsigned u)
{
    bits[u/32] |= (u+1) % 32;
    return *this;
}

Set256& Set256::operator -=(unsigned u)
{
    bits[u/32] -= (u+1) % 32;
    return *this;
}
```

```
Set256 Set256::operator &(Set256& b)
{
    Set256 newSet(*this);

    newSet &= b;
    return newSet;
}

Set256 Set256::operator |(Set256& b)
{
    Set256 newSet(*this);

    newSet |= b;
    return newSet;
}

Set256 Set256::operator -(Set256& b)
{
    Set256 newSet(*this);

    newSet -= b;
    return newSet;
}

Set256& Set256::operator &=(Set256& b)
{
    int i;
    for(i = 0; i <= 256/ULONG_BITS; i++)
        bits[i] &= b.bits[i];
    return *this;
}

Set256& Set256::operator |=(Set256& b)
{
    int i;
    for(i = 0; i <= 256/ULONG_BITS; i++)
        bits[i] |= b.bits[i];
    return *this;
}

Set256& Set256::operator -=(Set256& b)
{
    int i;
    for(i = 0; i <= 256/ULONG_BITS; i++)
        bits[i] -= b.bits[i];
    return *this;
}
```

## Generic Bit Set

```
// This is the more generic form of the BitSet class - the
// macros provide the ability to create a bit set type for
// sets from 0 .. N-1 for arbitrary n.

#ifndef ULONG_BITS
#define ULONG_BITS (sizeof(unsigned long)*8)
#define ULONG_SHIFT 4    /* assumes 32 bit long */
#endif

#include <generic.h>

#ifdef BRAINDEAD_INLINER
extern void memor(unsigned long *, unsigned long *, int);
extern void memand(unsigned long *, unsigned long *, int);
extern void memsub(unsigned long *, unsigned long *, int);
#else
inline
void memor(unsigned long *s1, unsigned long *s2, int len)
{  for(int i = 0; i < len; i++)  s1[i] |= s2[i];   }
inline
void memand(unsigned long *s1, unsigned long *s2, int len)
{  for(int i = 0; i < len; i++)  s1[i] &= s2[i];   }
inline
void memsub(unsigned long *s1, unsigned long *s2, int len)
{  for(int i = 0; i < len; i++)  s1[i] -= s2[i];   }
#endif

#define MakeBitSet(size)                                         \
class name2(BitSet,size) {                                       \
    unsigned long bits[(size+ULONG_BITS)>>ULONG_SHIFT];         \
public:                                                          \
    name2(BitSet,size)()                                         \
        { memset(bits, 0, sizeof(bits)); }                       \
    name2(BitSet,size)()                                         \
        {  }                                                     \
                                                                 \
    name2(BitSet,size)& clear()                                  \
        { memset(bits, 0, sizeof(bits));                         \
          return *this;}                                         \
    name2(BitSet,size)& fill()                                   \
        { memset(bits, ~0, sizeof(bits));                        \
          return *this;}                                         \
                                                                 \
    /* assignment and initialization */                         \
    name2(BitSet,size)(name2(BitSet,size)& s)                    \
        { memcpy(bits, s.bits, sizeof(bits)) }                   \
    name2(BitSet,size)& operator=(name2(BitSet,size)& s)         \
        { memcpy(bits, s.bits, sizeof(bits));                    \
          return *this;}                                         \
```

```
    /* destructive versions */                                      \
    name2(BitSet,size)& operator &=(unsigned u)                     \
        { bits[u/32] &= (u+1) % 32;                                 \
          return *this; }                                           \
    name2(BitSet,size)& operator |=(unsigned u)                     \
        { bits[u/32] |= (u+1) % 32;                                 \
          return *this; }                                           \
    name2(BitSet,size)& operator -=(unsigned u)                     \
        { bits[u/32] &= ~((u+1) % 32);                              \
                                                                    \
    /* operations on elements */                                    \
    name2(BitSet,size) operator &(unsigned u)                       \
        { name2(BitSet,size) b(*this);                              \
          b &= u;                                                   \
          return b; }                                               \
    name2(BitSet,size) operator |(unsigned u)                       \
        { name2(BitSet,size) b(*this);                              \
          b |= u;                                                   \
          return b; }                                               \
    name2(BitSct,size) operator -(unsigned u)                       \
        { name2(BitSet,size) b(*this);                              \
          b -= u;                                                   \
          return b; }                                               \
                                                                    \
    /* operations on name2(BitSet,size)s */                         \
    name2(BitSet,size) operator &(name2(BitSet,size)& s)            \
        { name2(BitSet,size) b(*this);                              \
          b &= s;                                                   \
          return b; }                                               \
    name2(BitSet,size) operator |(name2(BitSet,size)& s)            \
        { name2(BitSet,size) b(*this);                              \
          b |= s;                                                   \
          return b; }                                               \
    name2(BitSet,size) operator -(name2(BitSet,size)& s)            \
        { name2(BitSet,size) b(*this);                              \
          b -= s;                                                   \
          return b; }                                               \
                                                                    \
    /* destructive versions */                                      \
    name2(BitSet,size)& operator &=(name2(BitSet,size)& s)          \
        { return *this += s; }                                      \
    name2(BitSet,size)& operator |=(name2(BitSet,size)& b)          \
        { memor(bits, b.bits, size/ULONG_BITS);                     \
          return *this; }                                           \
    name2(BitSet,size)& operator -=(name2(BitSet,size)& b)          \
        { memsub(bits, b.bits, size/ULONG_BITS);                    \
          return *this; }                                           \
} ;
```

## Singly Linked List Definition

```
// Single link class - base class for any object that
// needs to be part of a singly linked list.

class Link {
    friend class List;
 protected:
    Link *_next;
    Link *_prev;
 public:
    Link()
        { _next = _prev = 0; }
    virtual ~Link();
    Link *next()
        { return _next; }
    Link *prev()
        { return _prev; }
} ;

class List {
 protected:
    Link *_first;
    Link *_last;
 public:
    List()
        { _first = _last = 0; }
    virtual ~List();
    Link *last()
        { return _last; }
    Link *first()
        { return _first; }

    List& append(Link *);
    List& prepend(Link *);
    List& remove(Link *);

    List& push(Link *l)
        { return append(l); }
    Link *pop()
        { Link *l = _last;
          remove(_last);
          return l; }
    Link *top()
        { return _last; }
} ;
```

## Singly Linked List Implementation

```
List&
List::append(Link *l)
{
    if (_last) {
        _last->_next = l;
        l->_prev = _last;
    }
    else
        _first = l;

    _last = l;

    return *this;
}

List&
List::prepend(Link *l)
{
    if (_first) {
        _first->_prev = l;
        l->_next = _first;
    }
    else
        _last = l;

    _first = l;

    return *this;
}

List&
List::remove(Link *l)
{
    if (l == _first)
        _first = _first->_next;
    if (l == _last)
        _last = _last->_prev;

    if (l->_next) {
        l->_next->_prev = l->_prev;
        l->_next = 0;
    }
    if (l->_prev) {
        l->_prev->_next = l->_next;
        l->_prev = 0;
    }

    return *this;
}
```

```
Link::~Link()
{
    if (_next) _next->_prev = _prev;
    if (_prev) _prev->_next = _next;
    _next = 0;
    _prev = 0;
}
```

## Generic Singly Linked List

```
// Generic single link class - base class for any object that
// needs to be part of a singly linked list.  This version is
// strongly typed.

#define MakeLink(TYPE)                                          \
                                                               \
class name2(TYPE,Link) : public Link {                         \
 public:                                                        \
    name2(TYPE,Link)()                                          \
        : Link()                                                \
        { }                                                     \
    virtual ~name2(TYPE,Link)()                                 \
        { }                                                     \
    TYPE *next()                                                \
        { return (TYPE *) _next; }                              \
    TYPE *prev()                                                \
        { return (TYPE *) _prev; }                              \
} ;

#define MakeList(TYPE)                                          \
                                                               \
class name2(TYPE,List) : public List {                         \
 public:                                                        \
    name2(TYPE,List)()                                          \
        : List()                                                \
        {  }                                                    \
    virtual ~name2(TYPE,List)()                                 \
        { }                                                     \
    TYPE *last()                                                \
        { return (TYPE *) _last; }                              \
    TYPE *first()                                               \
        { return (TYPE *) _first; }                             \
                                                               \
    TYPE *pop()                                                 \
        { return (TYPE *) List::pop(); }                        \
    TYPE *top()                                                 \
        { return (TYPE *) _last; }                              \
} ;
```

## Generic Array

```
// This class simply acts exactly like a real array of the
// specified type. It is also the basis for the bounds checking
// version.

#define Array(type)   name2(Array,type)

#define MakeArray(ETYPE)                                              \
class Array(TYPE) {                                                   \
 protected:                                                           \
    int _sz;                                                          \
    TYPE *_contents;                                                  \
                                                                     \
 public:                                                              \
    Array(type)(int sz)                                              \
        {                                                            \
            _contents = new TYPE[sz];                                \
            _sz = sz;                                                 \
        }                                                            \
    ~Array(type)()                                                   \
        { delete _contents; }                                        \
                                                                     \
    init()                                                           \
        {                                                            \
            assert(!(_sz || _contents));                             \
            _sz = newSize;                                            \
            _contents = new TYPE[_sz];                               \
        }                                                            \
                                                                     \
    TYPE& operator[](int i)                                         \
        { return _contents[i]; }                                     \
                                                                     \
    operator TYPE *()                                               \
        { return _contents; }                                        \
                                                                     \
    TYPE *operator&()                                               \
        { return _contents; }                                        \
                                                                     \
    int size()                                                       \
        { return sizeof(TYPE) * _sz; }                              \
} ;
```

## Generic BoundedArray

```
// This macro defines an Array class that implements bounds
// checking.  This is particularly useful for developing new
// code, when bounds violations can be a source of annoying
// errors.

#define BoundedArray(TYPE) name2(BoundedArray,TYPE)

#define MakeBoundedArray(TYPE)                                      \
class BoundedArray(TYPE)                                            \
    : public Array(TYPE){                                          \
 public:                                                           \
    BoundedArray(TYPE)(int sz)                                     \
    : Array(TYPE)(sz)                                              \
        { }                                                        \
                                                                   \
    ~BoundedArray(TYPE)();                                         \
                                                                   \
    TYPE& operator[](int i)                                       \
        {                                                          \
            assert(i < _sz);                                       \
            return _contents[i];                                   \
        }                                                          \
} ;
```

## Binary Tree Definition

```cpp
// This class implements a binary tree whose keys are integers.

struct BinaryTreeNode {
    BinaryTreeNode *left, *right;
    int value;
public:
    BinaryTreeNode(int newValue)
        { left = right = 0;   value = newValue; }
    ~BinaryTreeNode()
        { }
} ;


class BinaryTree {
    BinaryTreeNode *root;
    void BinaryTree::deleteNode(BinaryTreeNode *node);
public:
    BinaryTree()
        { root = 0; }
    ~BinaryTree();

    virtual int insert(int value);
    virtual int remove(int value);
    int lookup(int value);
} ;
```

# Binary Tree Implementation

```
int
BinaryTree::lookup(int value)
{
    BinaryTreeNode *cur = root;
    while (cur) {
        if (cur->value == value)
            return 1;
        else if (cur->value < value)
            cur = cur->left;
        else
            cur = cur->right;
    }

    return 0;
}

int
BinaryTree::insert(int value)
{
    BinaryTreeNode **cur = &root;

    while (*cur) {
        if (value == (*cur)->value)
            return 0;
        else if (value < (*cur)->value)
            cur = &((*cur)->left);
        else
            cur = &((*cur)->right);
    }

    (*cur) = new BinaryTreeNode(value);
    return 1;
}

void BinaryTree::deleteNode(BinaryTreeNode *node)
{
    if (node->left)
        deleteNode(node->left);
    if (node->right)
        deleteNode(node->right);
    delete node;
}

BinaryTree::~BinaryTree()
{
    deleteNode(root);
}
```

## Generic Binary Tree Definition

```
// Generic version of the BinaryTree class.  At a slight run-time
// and memory penalty, this version of the class supports the use
// of arbitrary keys

struct BinaryTreeNode {
    BinaryTreeNode *left, *right;
    void *value;
public:
    BinaryTreeNode(void *newValue)
        { left = right = 0;   value = newValue; }
    ~BinaryTreeNode()
        { }
} ;

typedef int (*ComparisonFunction)(void *, void *);

class BinaryTree {
    BinaryTreeNode *root;
    ComparisonFunction  _compare;
public:
    BinaryTree(ComparisonFunction compare)
        { root = 0; _compare = compare; }
    ~BinaryTree();

    virtual void *insert(void *value);
    virtual int remove(int value);
    void *lookup(void *value);
} ;
```

## Generic Binary Tree Implementation

```
// Generic version of the BinaryTree class.  At a slight run-time
// and memory penalty, this version of the class supports the use
// of arbitrary keys

void *
BinaryTree::lookup(void *value)
{
    BinaryTreeNode *cur = root;
    while (cur) {
        int result = (*_compare)(cur->value, value);
        if (!result)
            return cur->valuc;
        else if (result < 0)
            cur = cur->left;
        else
            cur = cur->right;
    }

    return 0;
}

void *
BinaryTree::insert(void *value)
{
    BinaryTreeNode **cur = &root;

    while (*cur) {
        int result = (*_compare)(value, (*cur)->value);
        if (result == 0)
            return (*cur)->value;
        else if (result < 0)
            cur = &((*cur)->left);
        else
            cur = &((*cur)->right);
    }

    (*cur) = new BinaryTreeNode(value);
    return value;
}
```

## HashTable Definition

```
// Like the basic BinaryTree class, this class provides a
// mechanism for tracking items with integer keys.

struct HashEntry {
    unsigned long key;      /* hash key */
    void        *value;
    HashEntry     *next, *prev;

    /* if this is inline, redundant sets of next, prev, and
     * refcount should peephole out */
    HashEntry(unsigned long newkey)
        { key = newkey; next = 0; prev = 0; }
    ~HashEntry()
        {
            if (next) next->prev = prev;
            if (prev) prev->next = next;
        }
} ;

typedef HashEntry* HashEntryPtr;

const NBUCKETS=4096;

/* much of this borrowed from Phil's X code. */
class HashTable {
    HashEntryPtr bucket[NBUCKETS];

    HashEntryPtr addElement(unsigned long key);
    HashEntryPtr searchBucketFor(HashEntryPtr p,
                                 unsigned long key);
    hash(unsigned long);

public:
    HashTable();
    ~HashTable();
    void add(unsigned long key, void *value);
    void *lookup(unsigned long key);
    void remove(unsigned long key);
    void mapcar(void (*f)(HashEntryPtr));
} ;
```

# HashTable Implementation

```
#include <osfcn.h>
#include "HashTable.h"

unsigned const RESOURCE_ID_MASK = 0xfffff;

HashTable::HashTable()
{
    for(int i = 0; i < NBUCKETS; i++)
        bucket[i] = 0;
}

HashTable::~HashTable()
{
    for(int i = 0; i < NBUCKETS; i++) {
        HashEntryPtr p = bucket[i];

        while(p) {
            bucket[i] = p->next;
            delete p;
            p = bucket[i];
        }
    }
}

int
HashTable::hash(register unsigned long key)
{
    unsigned const RESOURCE_ID_MASK = 0xfffff;

    key &= RESOURCE_ID_MASK;

    return ((int)(0x7FF & (key ^ (key>>11)))));
}

void *
HashTable::lookup(register unsigned long key)
{
    int whichBucket = hash(key);

    HashEntryPtr p = searchBucketFor(bucket[whichBucket], key);

    if (!p)
        return 0;

    return p->value;
}
```

```
void
HashTable::mapcar(void (*f)(HashEntryPtr))
{
    for(int i = 0; i < NBUCKETS; i++) {
        HashEntryPtr p = bucket[i];

        while(p) {
            f(p);
            p = p->next;
        }
    }
}


HashEntryPtr
HashTable::searchBucketFor(register HashEntryPtr p,
                           register unsigned long key)
{
    while(p) {
        if (p->key == key)
            break;
        p = p->next;
    }
    return p;
}


HashEntryPtr
HashTable::addElement(register unsigned long key)
{
    int whichBucket = hash(key);

    HashEntryPtr p = new HashEntry(key);

    p->next = bucket[whichBucket];
    if (bucket[whichBucket])
        bucket[whichBucket]->prev = p;
    bucket[whichBucket] = p;

    return p;
}
```

```
void
HashTable::add(register unsigned long key, void *value)
{
    int whichBucket = hash(key);

    HashEntryPtr p = searchBucketFor(bucket[whichBucket], key);

    if (p)
        abort();

    p = addElement(key);
    p->value = value;
}

void
HashTable::remove(unsigned long key)
{
    int whichBucket = hash(key);

    HashEntryPtr p = searchBucketFor(bucket[whichBucket], key);
    if(!p)
        return;

    if(bucket[whichBucket] == p)
        bucket[whichBucket] = p->next;

    delete p;
}
```

## Generic HashTable Definition

```
// Generic hashtable class

#include <generic.h>

#ifndef NBUCKETS
#define NBUCKETS 4096
#endif

#define HashTable(KEYTYPE) name2(HashTable_,KEYTYPE)
#define HashEntry(KEYTYPE) name2(HashEntry_,KEYTYPE)
#define HashEntryPtr(KEYTYPE) name2(HashEntryPtr_,KEYTYPE)

#define MakeHashTable(KEYTYPE)                               \
struct HashEntry(KEYTYPE) {                                  \
    KEYTYPE             key;  /* hash key */                 \
    void                *value;                              \
    HashEntry(KEYTYPE) *next, *prev;                         \
                                                             \
    HashEntry(KEYTYPE)(KEYTYPE newkey)                       \
        { key = newkey; next = 0; prev = 0; }               \
    ~HashEntry(KEYTYPE)()                                    \
        {                                                    \
            if (next) next->prev = prev;                     \
            if (prev) prev->next = next;                     \
        }                                                    \
} ;                                                          \
                                                             \
typedef HashEntry(KEYTYPE)* HashEntryPtr(KEYTYPE);           \
                                                             \
class HashTable(KEYTYPE) {                                   \
    HashEntryPtr(KEYTYPE) bucket[NBUCKETS];                  \
                                                             \
    int (*_compare)(KEYTYPE, KEYTYPE);                       \
    HashEntryPtr(KEYTYPE) addElement(KEYTYPE key);           \
    HashEntryPtr(KEYTYPE)                                    \
        searchBucketFor(HashEntryPtr(KEYTYPE) p,             \
                        KEYTYPE key);                        \
    int hash(KEYTYPE);                                       \
public:                                                      \
    HashTable(KEYTYPE)(int (*)(KEYTYPE, KEYTYPE));           \
    ~HashTable(KEYTYPE)();                                   \
    void add(KEYTYPE key, void * value);                    \
    void *lookup(KEYTYPE key);                               \
    void remove(KEYTYPE key);                                \
    void mapcar(void (*f)(HashEntryPtr(KEYTYPE)));           \
} ;
```

```
#define ImplementHashTable(KEYTYPE)                              \
HashTable(KEYTYPE)::HashTable(KEYTYPE)                           \
            (int (*compare)(KEYTYPE, KEYTYPE))                  \
{                                                               \
    _compare = compare;                                         \
    for(int i = 0; i < NBUCKETS; i++)                           \
        bucket[i] = 0;                                          \
}                                                               \
                                                                \
HashTable(KEYTYPE)::~HashTable(KEYTYPE)()                       \
{                                                               \
    for(int i = 0; i < NBUCKETS; i++) {                        \
        HashEntryPtr(KEYTYPE) p = bucket[i];                    \
                                                                \
        while(p) {                                              \
            bucket[i] = p->next;                                \
            delete p;                                           \
            p = bucket[i];                                      \
        }                                                       \
    }                                                           \
}                                                               \
void *                                                          \
HashTable(KEYTYPE)::lookup(register KEYTYPE key)                \
{                                                               \
    int whichBucket = hash(key);                                \
                                                                \
    register HashEntryPtr(KEYTYPE) p =                          \
        searchBucketFor(bucket[whichBucket], key);             \
    if (!p)                                                     \
        return 0;                                               \
                                                                \
    return p->value;                                            \
}                                                               \
                                                                \
void                                                            \
HashTable(KEYTYPE)::mapcar(void (*f)(HashEntryPtr(KEYTYPE)))    \
{                                                               \
    for(int i = 0; i < NBUCKETS; i++) {                        \
        HashEntryPtr(KEYTYPE) p = bucket[i];                    \
                                                                \
        while(p) {                                              \
            f(p);                                               \
            p = p->next;                                        \
        }                                                       \
    }                                                           \
}                                                               \
```

```
HashEntryPtr(KEYTYPE)                                               \
HashTable(KEYTYPE)::searchBucketFor(HashEntryPtr(KEYTYPE) p,        \
                                    register KEYTYPE key)           \
{                                                                   \
    while(p) {                                                      \
        if (_compare(p->key,key) == 0)                             \
            break;                                                  \
        p = p->next;                                                \
    }                                                               \
    return p;                                                       \
}                                                                   \
                                                                    \
HashEntryPtr(KEYTYPE)                                               \
HashTable(KEYTYPE)::addElement(register KEYTYPE key)                \
                                                                    \
{                                                                   \
    int whichBucket = hash(key);                                    \
                                                                    \
    HashEntryPtr(KEYTYPE) p = new HashEntry(KEYTYPE)(key);          \
                                                                    \
                                                                    \
    p->next = bucket[whichBucket];                                  \
    if (bucket[whichBucket])                                        \
        bucket[whichBucket]->prev = p;                              \
    bucket[whichBucket] = p;                                        \
                                                                    \
    return p;                                                       \
}                                                                   \
                                                                    \
void                                                                \
HashTable(KEYTYPE)::add(register KEYTYPE key, void *value)          \
                                                                    \
{                                                                   \
    int whichBucket = hash(key);                                    \
                                                                    \
    HashEntryPtr(KEYTYPE) p =                                       \
        searchBucketFor(bucket[whichBucket], key);                 \
                                                                    \
    if (p)                                                          \
        abort();                                                    \
                                                                    \
    p = addElement(key);                                            \
    p->value = value;                                               \
}                                                                   \
                                                                    \
```

```
void                                                                    \
HashTable(KEYTYPE)::remove(KEYTYPE key)                                 \
{                                                                        \
    int whichBucket = hash(key);                                        \
                                                                         \
    HashEntryPtr(KEYTYPE) p =                                           \
        searchBucketFor(bucket[whichBucket], key);                     \
    if(!p)                                                              \
        return;                                                         \
                                                                         \
        bucket[whichBucket] = p->next;                                  \
                                                                         \
    delete p;                                                           \
}
```

## Generic HashTable Implementation

```
// Sample implementation of a generic hash table.

#include "HashTable.gen.h"

typedef unsigned long u_long;
extern "C" int abort(void);

MakeHashTable(u_long);

ImplementHashTable(u_long);

int
HashTable(u_long)::hash(register u_long key)
{
    unsigned const RESOURCE_ID_MASK = 0xffffff;

    key &= RESOURCE_ID_MASK;

    return ((int)(0x7FF & (key ^ (key>>11))));
}
```

# Generic Pointer

```
// This macro constructs a class that behaves just like a normal
// pointer.  It is the basis of the reference-counted pointer
// class.

#include <generic.h>
#define Ptr(T)   name2(Pointer_,T)

#define MakePtr(T)                                                  \
    friend delete(Ptr(T)&)                                         \
class Ptr(T) {                                                     \
    T *_ptr;                                                        \
                                                                   \
 public:                                                            \
    Ptr(T)()                                                        \
       { _ptr = 0; }                                               \
    Ptr(T)(T *t)                                                    \
       { _ptr - t; }                                               \
    Ptr(T)(Ptr(T)& pt)                                             \
       { _ptr = pt._ptr; }                                        \
                                                                   \
    T *ptr()                                                        \
       { return _ptr; }                                            \
    operator T *()                                                 \
       { return _ptr; }                                            \
                                                                   \
    operator int()                                                 \
       { return (int) _ptr; }                                     \
    int operator !()                                               \
       { return !_ptr; }                                          \
                                                                   \
    Ptr(T)& operator=(Ptr(T)& pt)                                 \
       { _ptr = pt._ptr; }                                        \
    Ptr(T)& operator=(T *t);                                       \
       { _ptr = t; }                                              \
                                                                   \
    T *operator->()                                                \
       { return _ptr; };                                          \
    T& operator*()                                                 \
       { return *_ptr; };                                         \
} ;
```

# Reference Counting Pointer

```
// These classes implement the necessary logic for building
// reference counted objects and the associated pointers.

class Counted {
    friend class RPtr;
    int nreferences;     // number of references to this object
    addRef()
        { nreferences++; }
    delRef()
        {
            if (--nreferences)
              delete this;
        }
  public:
    Counted()
        { nreferences = 0; }
    ~Counted();
} ;

class RPtr_base {
  protected:
    Counted *ptr;
    RPtr_base()
        { ptr = 0; }
    RPtr(RPtr& r)
        { ptr = r.ptr;
          if(ptr) ptr->addref();
          return *this;
        }
    RPtr(Counted *tp)
        { ptr = tp;
          if(ptr) ptr->addref();
          return *this;
        }

    ~RPtr()
        { if (ptr)  ptr->delref(); }

    RPtr& operator=(RPtr& r)
        { if (ptr) ptr->delref();
          ptr = r.ptr;
          if(ptr) ptr->addref();
          return *this;
        }
```

```
        RPtr& operator=(Counted *tp)
            { if (ptr) ptr->delref();
              ptr = tp;
              if(ptr) ptr->addref();
              return *this;
            }
} ;

#define RPtr(T) name2(Rptr_,T)

#define MakeRPtr(T)                                       \
class RPtr(T) : public RPtr_base {                        \
    Counted *ptr;                                         \
  public:                                                 \
    RPtr(T)()                                             \
        : RPtr_base()                                     \
        { }                                               \
    RPtr(T)(RPtr(T)& r)                                   \
        : RPtr_base(r)                                    \
        { }                                               \
    RPtr(T)(T *tp)                                        \
        : RPtr_base((Counted *) T)                        \
        { }                                               \
    ~RPtr(T)()                                            \
        { }                                               \
                                                          \
    RPtr(T)& operator=(RPtr(T)& r)                        \
        { *((RPtr_base *) this) = r; }                    \
    RPtr(T)& operator=(T *tp)                             \
        { *((RPtr_base *) this) =                         \
                (Counted *) tp; }                         \
                                                          \
    T& operator *()                                       \
        { assert(ptr); return *((T *) ptr); }             \
    T *operator->()                                       \
        { assert(ptr); return (T *) ptr; }                \
                                                          \
    operator T *()                                        \
        { return (T *) ptr; }                             \
    int operator !()                                      \
        { return !ptr; }                                  \
} ;
```

## NameSpace Definition

```
// The NameSpace class implements name management with atoms.
// It provides interning and lookup mechanisms.

#pragma once
// Depends on the generic binary tree implementation:
#include "BinaryTree.h"

typedef unsigned long Atom;

/*
 * You pass in a pointer to the function that makes the
 * predeclared atoms:
 */
class NameSpace;
typedef int (*AtomCreFun)(NameSpace *);
typedef unsigned long Atom;
const Atom NullAtom = 0;

// until C++ properly supports nesting, these must unfortunately
// be at top level...

struct StringNode {
    int signature;
    char *string;
} ;

struct AtomNode : public StringNode {
    Atom atomValue;
} ;

class NameSpace {
    Atom nextAtomValue;
    BinaryTree nodes;
    char **stringTable;
    int tableLength;

    void growTable();
public:
    NameSpace();
    ~NameSpace();

    Atom intern(char *);
    Atom lookup(char *);
    char *atomName(Atom);
} ;
```

# NameSpace Implementation

```
#include <string.h>
#include "NameSpace.h"

static int
CompareAtomStrings(void *v1, void *v2)
{
    StringNode *s1 = (StringNode *) v1, *s2 = (StringNode *) v2;

    if (s1->signature != s2->signature)
        return s1->signature - s2->signature;
    return strcmp(s1->string, s2->string);
}

NameSpace::NameSpace()
    : nodes(CompareAtomStrings)
{
    tableLength = 128;
    stringTable = new char *[128];
    stringTable[NullAtom] = 0;
}

static int
StringSignature(char * string)
{
    int i;
    int len = strlen(string);
    int signature = 0;

    for (i = 0; i < (len+1)/2; i++)
    {
        signature = signature * 27 + string[i];
        signature = signature * 27 + string[len - 1 - i];
    }

    return signature;
}

void
NameSpace::growTable()
{
    int newTableLength = 2 * tableLength;
    char **newTable = new char *[newTableLength];
    for (int i = 0; i < tableLength; i++)
        newTable[i] = stringTable[i];
    delete stringTable;
    stringTable = newTable;
}
```

```
Atom
NameSpace::intern(char *s)
{
    AtomNode *anp = new AtomNode;
    AtomNode *oldanp;

    anp->signature = StringSignature(s);
    anp->string = s;

    oldanp = (AtomNode *) nodes.insert(anp);
    if (oldanp != anp) {
        delete anp;
        return oldanp->atomValue;
    }

    anp->atomValue = nextAtomValue++;
    if (anp->atomValue >= tableLength)
        growTable();

    char * str = new char[strlen(s)+1];
    strcpy(str, s);

    stringTable[anp->atomValue] = str;
    return anp->atomValue;
}

Atom
NameSpace::lookup(char *s)
{
    AtomNode *anp;
    StringNode sn;

    sn.signature = StringSignature(s);
    sn.string = s;

    anp = (AtomNode *) nodes.lookup(&sn);

    if (anp)
        return anp->atomValue;

    return NullAtom;
}

char *
NameSpace::atomName(Atom atom)
{
    return stringTable[atom];
}
```

# Index